STORMS,
VIOLENT WINDS,
AND EARTH'S ATMOSPHERE

DYNAMIC EARTH

STORMS,
VIOLENT WINDS,
AND EARTH'S ATMOSPHERE

EDITED BY JOHN P. RAFFERTY, ASSOCIATE EDITOR, EARTH SCIENCES

Educational Publishing

IN ASSOCIATION WITH

EDUCATIONAL SERVICES

Published in 2011 by Britannica Educational Publishing
(a trademark of Encyclopædia Britannica, Inc.)
in association with Rosen Educational Services, LLC
29 East 21st Street, New York, NY 10010.

First Edition

Britannica Educational Publishing
Michael I. Levy: Executive Editor
J.E. Luebering: Senior Manager
Marilyn L. Barton: Senior Coordinator, Production Control
Steven Bosco: Director, Editorial Technologies
Lisa S. Braucher: Senior Producer and Data Editor
Yvette Charboneau: Senior Copy Editor
Kathy Nakamura: Manager, Media Acquisition
John P. Rafferty: Associate Editor, Earth Sciences

Rosen Educational Services
Jeanne Nagle: Senior Editor
Joanne Randolph: Editor
Nelson Sá: Art Director
Cindy Reiman: Photography Manager
Nicole Russo: Designer
Matthew Cauli: Cover Design
Introduction by Michael Raymond

Library of Congress Cataloging-in-Publication Data

Storms, violent winds, and earth's atmosphere / edited by John P. Rafferty.—1st ed.
    p. cm.—(Dynamic earth)
"In association with Britannica Educational Publishing, Rosen Educational Services."
Includes bibliographical references and index.
ISBN 978-1-61530-114-0 (library binding)
1. Storms. 2. Winds. 3. Atmosphere. I. Rafferty, John P.
QC941.S757 2010
551.55—dc22

                                                              2009049109

Manufactured in the United States of America

CONTENTS

25

33

42

43

65

75

80

83

113

121

134

142

154

188

207

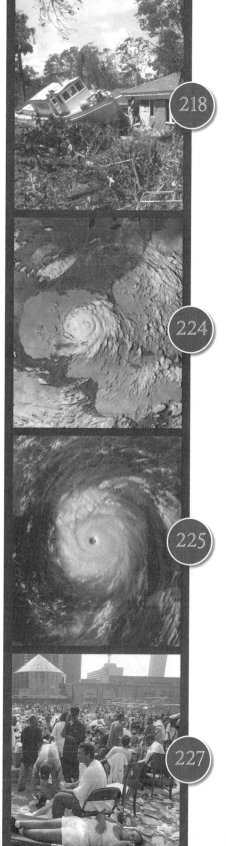

INTRODUCTION

Anyone who has ever been caught in a severe storm will be able to tell you a little bit about the awesome power of inclement weather. Most people have had a personal experience with severe weather. Perhaps swirling winds have downed a tree on their street, or lightning has struck the roof of a neighbor's house. Tornadoes, hurricanes (the North American name for tropical cyclones), thunderstorms, and violent winds all are capable of devastating one's immediate physical surroundings. Time and time again, stories about such storms serve as useful reminders that the weather, especially in its most violent forms, demands respect and attention at all times.

While readers are undoubtedly familiar with a storm's awe-inspiring capacity to inflict damage, they might know significantly less about how such events originate in our atmosphere, how they are classified, and how scientists track and predict them. This volume details the patterns and tendencies of wind-related storms, and offers historical examples that vividly illustrate the havoc nature can wreak.

The life cycle of any given weather system begins long before most of its damaging properties can be detected. High winds, hurricanes, and tornadoes begin as subtle atmospheric processes. Indeed, each kind of storm relies on a particular set of atmospheric conditions in order to form.

Atmospheric temperature is one of the many vital factors in the formation of storms and weather systems. Variations in temperature help determine which way air will flow in the atmosphere, and thus have a substantial impact on atmospheric pressure. Typically, inclement weather is associated with low pressure at Earth's surface, while high pressure usually indicates clearer, drier conditions.

The temperature at the interface of the atmosphere and Earth's surface is a result of three processes: radiation, conduction, and convection. This interface is considered to be a part of the troposphere, the lowest level of the earth's atmosphere and the place where most of earth's weather occurs. The troposphere comprises part of the vertical structure of the earth's atmosphere. To a degree, events occurring within the troposphere influence the behaviour of air in the layers above. Equally important in the formation of weather systems is the distribution of heat across the horizontal structure of the Earth's atmosphere. This dimension is largely dependent on the amount and distribution of solar radiation that comes in contact with the planet. Affected by Earth's rotation and axial tilt, the distribution of heat from the Sun across the globe is consistent and relatively predictable over the course of a year. The circulation of air across the horizontal structure of the atmosphere follows a similarly consistent pattern as a result, transporting heat from the latitudes of highest solar insolation to the latitudes of lowest heating. Clouds, which are formed by the lifting and expansion of damp air as it moves upwards and into areas of lower atmosphere pressure, can be good indicators of imminent bad weather. At their most basic level, clouds indicate a high level of moisture in the atmosphere. As this moisture accumulates, condensation occurs on particles in the air and clouds form. Precipitation can occur soon after, thereby returning moisture to Earth's surface in the form of drizzle, rain, snow, snow pellets, ice crystals, or hail.

Precipitation on its own is not necessarily a notable event. When strong winds are added to the picture, however, the propensity for damaging weather becomes more likely. Winds are largely the result of horizontal and vertical differences in atmospheric pressure, but at smaller, more localized scales, various topographic features significantly influence wind systems, which play a large role in determining local climates and weather. Because there are many different types of winds, a classification scale has been developed based on the size and scope of wind systems. Wind systems are place in the planetary scale, the synoptic scale, and the mesoscale. The planetary scale includes the largest and longest-lived wind systems on Earth, whereas the synoptic scale refers to winds that are influenced heavily by the horizontal structure of the atmosphere and typically span smaller distances and have shorter lifetimes. Synoptic-scale winds include the infamous trade winds and the westerlies. The third wind classification is the mesoscale, whose winds include less intense local systems, tornadoes, and thunderstorms.

The speed and force of winds in a given weather system are important tools in classifying these systems, especially when referring to cyclones and tornadoes. Though it is common to call any inclement weather system a storm, the meteorological term "storm" is reserved for a cyclone with a strong low-pressure center and winds ranging from 103 to 117 kilometres (64 to 73 miles) per hour. Storms also are characterized by heavy precipitation, and, at times, lightning and thunder. Windstorms, however, have less stringent requirements. They are defined simply as a wind that is strong enough to cause light damage to trees or buildings. These types of storms include monsoons and cyclones.

Monsoons are seasonal winds that change direction from summer to winter and are determined by contrasts in land and sea temperatures. These phenomena originate over cool regions and blow toward warmer areas. The most well-known monsoon occurs in India and southeast

Asia, although Australia and Africa have also been affected by such storms. Conditions that allow the development of monsoonal systems exist in Europe and North America as well, but these usually dissipate into fierce thunderstorms rather than true monsoons. The damage that these storm systems inflict is not restricted to strong winds. Summer monsoons are frequently accompanied by tremendous amounts of rain that can cause flooding and landslides.

Cyclones, which are defined as large wind systems that circulate about a centre of low atmospheric pressure, are one of the planet's most amazing phenomena. North of the equator, cyclones rotate inward in a counterclockwise direction. South of the equator, they rotate clockwise. Anticyclonal systems occur in similar areas as cyclones; however, they spiral outward from a high-pressure center and rotate in the opposite directions of cyclones north and south of the equator. Typically, cyclones are associated with heavy precipitation, while anticyclones are often weaker and dryer systems.

Cyclones are divided into two different classes: extratropical and tropical. Tropical cyclones, also known as typhoons or hurricanes, typically form over warm tropical oceans. They begin as tropical storms, with sustained surface winds of 63 to 118 kilometres (39 to 73 miles) per hour. When wind speeds exceed 119 kilometres (74 miles) per hour, the storm is reclassified as a tropical cyclone. Along with high winds and heavy rains, tropical cyclones may be accompanied by a storm surge, which is an elevation of the sea surface that can pose a serious threat to coastal areas.

The intensity of a tropical cyclone can be measured on two different scales, both ranging from 1 to 5, depending on where the storm occurs. Hurricanes in the Atlantic and Pacific are measured on the Saffir-Simpson hurricane scale, while storms near Australia are categorized on a slightly different scale. On both scales, category 5 hurricanes are considered to be the most serious storms with the greatest potential to cause significant damage and loss of life. Category 5 hurricanes occurring in the United States have included the Galveston hurricane of 1900, Hurricane Camille in 1969, Hurricane Andrew in 1992, and most recently, Hurricane Katrina in 2005.

Extratropical cyclones, also known as wave cyclones, originate in middle or high latitudes. Unlike tropical cyclones, extratropical cyclones form as a result of horizontal temperature gradients called frontal zones. These cyclones are typically less intense than their tropical counterparts.

Thunderstorms, which can emerge from both tropical and extratropical cyclones, happen in almost every region of the world. Like cyclones, they also are associated with high winds. Thunderstorms develop when a mass of warm, moist air rises swiftly and comes into contact with the cooler portions of the atmosphere in what is known as an updraft. This movement of air creates clouds, precipitation, and columns of cooled air. These columns then descend back toward Earth's surface in a downdraft, producing gusts of high winds. As this interplay between updrafts and downdrafts occurs, cloud particles acquire electrical charges in a process called electricification. These charges, in turn, produce lightning. As the lightning surges and heats the surrounding air, it creates shock waves due to sharp changes in pressure, better known as thunder.

Thunderstorms are classified by their intensity and size. They range from isolated and multiple-cell storms to supercell storms. Supercell storms have some of the most unique and intense properties. In some instances, they may even spawn tornadoes.

Tornadoes typically occur in the mid-latitudes of the Northern and Southern Hemispheres. These areas of the globe are at the highest risk of experiencing the dangers associated with tornadoes, which can include tangential wind speeds of 125 to 160 metres per second (about 410 to 525 feet per second) or 450 to 575 kilometres per hour (280 to 360 miles per hour). Tornadoes produce some of the strongest winds known to occur near Earth's surface. These devastating winds are the reason so much attention is paid to tornado detection and prediction.

Human beings spend a great deal of time studying Earth's fascinating weather systems and the processes that fuel them. Through this study we can gain perspective on the interconnectedness of weather systems in Earth's atmosphere. Since weather is a constant of each person's daily life, understanding its causes, effects, and other related factors is a useful and important undertaking. The ability to predict when violent storms will strike, as well as their intensity when they do, has saved countless lives. More than that, as readers of this book will discover, the study of storms provides additional insight into the dynamic natural processes in play on planet Earth.

Chapter 1

THE ROLE OF THE ATMOSPHERE

People witness the effects of weather occurring in Earth's atmosphere daily. It is true that rain and snow provide water for crops, drinking, washing, and other activities. However, driven by aggressive winds, rain can fall in torrents and gently falling snow can become a blizzard. Occasionally, the forces that produce Earth's weather can even generate destructive tornadoes and tropical cyclones. Indeed, phenomena occurring within Earth's thin atmosphere may be every bit as violent and destructive as the processes that take place beneath its surface. However, violent weather is observed by people much more frequently than earthquakes and volcanoes. To fully understand how violent weather is produced, one must know how Earth's atmosphere works.

EARTH'S ATMOSPHERE

Atmospheres are gas and aerosol (microscopic suspended particles of dust, soot, smoke, or chemicals) envelopes that extend from the ocean, land, and ice-covered surface of planets outward into space. The density of the atmosphere decreases outward, because the gravitational attraction of the planet, which pulls the gases and aerosols inward, is greatest close to the surface. Atmospheres of some planetary bodies, such as Mercury, are almost nonexistent, as the primordial atmosphere has escaped the relatively low gravitational attraction of the planet and has been released into space. Other planets, such as Venus, Earth, Mars, and the giant outer planets of the solar system, have retained an atmosphere. In addition, Earth's atmosphere has been able to contain water in each of its three phases (solid, liquid, and gas), which has been essential for the development of life on the planet.

The evolution of Earth's current atmosphere is not completely understood. It is thought that the current atmosphere resulted from a gradual release of gases both from the planet's interior and from the metabolic activities of life-forms—as opposed to the primordial atmosphere, which developed by outgassing (venting) during the original formation of the planet. Current volcanic gaseous emissions include water vapour (H_2O), carbon dioxide (CO_2), sulfur dioxide (SO_2), hydrogen sulfide (H_2S), carbon monoxide (CO), chlorine (Cl), fluorine (F), and diatomic nitrogen (N_2; consisting of two atoms in a single molecule), as well as traces of other substances. Approximately 85 percent of volcanic emissions are in the form of water vapour. In contrast, carbon dioxide is about 10 percent of the effluent.

During the early evolution of the atmosphere on Earth, water must have been able to exist as a liquid, since the oceans have been present for at least three billion years. Given that solar output four billion years ago was only about 60 percent of what it is today, enhanced levels of carbon dioxide and perhaps ammonia (NH_3) must have been present in order to retard the loss of infrared radiation into space. The initial life-forms that evolved in this environment must have been anaerobic (i.e., surviving in the absence of oxygen). In addition, they must have been able to resist the biologically destructive ultraviolet radiation in sunlight, which was not absorbed by a layer of ozone as it is now.

Once organisms developed the capability for photosynthesis, oxygen was produced in large quantities. The buildup of oxygen in the atmosphere also permitted the development of the ozone layer as O_2 molecules were dissociated into monatomic oxygen (O; consisting of single oxygen atoms) and recombined with other O_2 molecules to form triatomic ozone molecules (O_3). The capability for photosynthesis arose in primitive forms of plants between two and three billion years ago. Previous to the evolution of photosynthetic organisms, oxygen was produced in limited quantities as a by-product of the decomposition of water vapour by ultraviolet radiation.

The current molecular composition of Earth's atmosphere is diatomic nitrogen (N_2), 78.08 percent; diatomic oxygen (O_2), 20.95 percent; argon (A), 0.93 percent; water (H_2O), about 0 to 4 percent; and carbon dioxide (CO_2), 0.038 percent. Inert gases such as neon (Ne), helium (He), and krypton (Kr) and other constituents such as nitrogen oxides, compounds of sulfur, and compounds of ozone are found in lesser amounts.

THE ENERGY BUDGET OF EARTH'S ATMOSPHERE

The flow of energy from the Sun to Earth and the outflow of energy from Earth is called the energy budget. Earth's atmosphere is bounded at the bottom by water and land—that is, by the surface of Earth. Heating of this surface is accomplished by three physical processes—radiation, conduction, and convection—and the temperature at the interface of the atmosphere and surface is a result of this heating.

The relative contributions of each process depend on the wind, temperature, and moisture structure in the atmosphere immediately above the surface, the intensity of solar insolation, and the physical characteristics of the surface. The temperature occurring at this interface is of critical importance in determining how suitable a location is for different forms of life. The following sections will further explain the processes of radiation, conduction, and convection, which all play a part in Earth's energy budget.

RADIATION

The temperature of the atmosphere and surface is influenced by electromagnetic radiation, and this radiation is traditionally divided into two types: insolation from the Sun and emittance from the surface and the atmosphere. Insolation is frequently referred to as shortwave radiation. It falls primarily within the ultraviolet and visible portions of the electromagnetic spectrum and consists predominantly of wavelengths of 0.39 to 0.76 micrometres (0.00002 to 0.00003 inch). Radiation emitted from Earth is called longwave radiation. It falls within the infrared portion of the spectrum and has typical wavelengths of 4 to 30 micrometres (0.0002 to 0.001 inch). Wavelengths of radiation emitted by a body depend on the temperature of the body, as specified by Planck's radiation law. The Sun, with its surface temperature of around 6,000 kelvins (K; about 5,725 °C, or 10,337 °F), emits at a much shorter wavelength than does Earth, which has lower surface and atmospheric temperatures around 250 to 300 K (-23 to 27 °C, or -9.4 to 80.6 °F).

A fraction of the incoming shortwave radiation is absorbed by atmospheric gases, including water vapour,

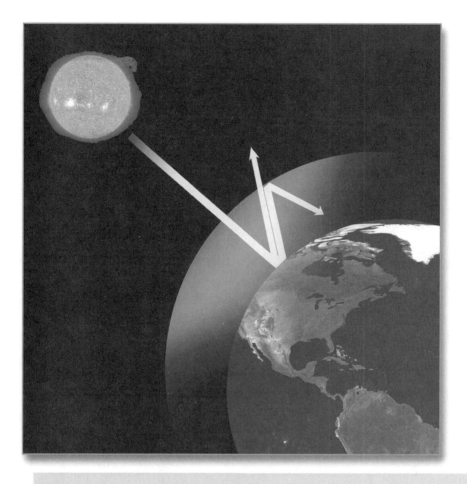

Illustration of the greenhouse effect, which is the process by which heat gets trapped in the atmosphere. Photo Researchers, Inc.

and warms the air directly, but in the absence of clouds most of this energy reaches the surface. The scattering of a fraction of the shortwave radiation—particularly of the shortest wavelengths by air molecules in a process called Rayleigh scattering—produces Earth's blue skies.

When tall thick clouds are present, a large percentage (up to about 80 percent) of the insolation is reflected back into space. (The fraction of reflected shortwave radiation is called the cloud albedo.) Of the solar radiation reaching Earth's surface, some is reflected back into the atmosphere. Values of the surface albedo range as high as 0.95 for fresh snow to 0.10 for dark, organic soils. On land, this reflection occurs entirely at the surface. In water, however, albedo depends on the angle of the Sun's rays and the depth of the water column. If the Sun's rays strike the water surface at an oblique angle, albedo may be higher than 0.85. If these rays are more direct, only a small portion, perhaps as low as 0.02, is reflected, while the rest of the insolation is scattered within the water column and absorbed. Shortwave radiation penetrates a volume of water to significant depths (up to several hundred metres [feet]) before the insolation is completely attenuated. The heating by solar radiation in water is distributed through a depth, which results in smaller temperature changes at the surface of the water than would occur with the same insolation over an equal area of land.

The amount of solar radiation reaching the surface depends on latitude, time of year, time of day, and orientation of the land surface with respect to the Sun. In the Northern Hemisphere north of 23°30′, for example, solar insolation at local noon is less on slopes facing the north than on land oriented toward the south.

Solar radiation is made up of direct and diffuse radiation. Direct shortwave radiation reaches the surface without being absorbed or scattered from its line of propagation by the intervening atmosphere. The image of the Sun's disk as a sharp and distinct object represents that portion of the solar radiation that reaches the viewer directly. Diffuse radiation, in contrast, reaches the surface after first being scattered from its line of propagation. On an overcast day, for example, the Sun's disk is not visible, and all of the shortwave radiation is diffuse.

Long-wave radiation is emitted by the atmosphere and propagates both upward and downward. According to the Stefan-Boltzmann law, the total amount of long-wave energy emitted is proportional to the fourth power of the temperature of the emitting material (e.g., the ground surface or the atmospheric layer). The magnitude of this radiation reaching the surface depends on the temperature at the height of emission and the amount of absorption that takes place between the height of emission and the surface. A larger fraction of the long-wave radiation is absorbed when the intervening atmosphere holds large amounts of water vapour and carbon dioxide. Clouds with liquid water concentrations near 2.5 grams per cubic metre absorb almost 100 percent of the long-wave radiation within a depth of 12 metres (40 feet) into the cloud. Clouds with lower liquid water concentrations require greater depths before complete absorption is attained (e.g., a cloud with a water content of 0.05 gram per cubic metre requires about 600 metres [about 2,000 feet] for complete absorption). Clouds that are at least this thick emit long-wave radiation from their bases downward to Earth's surface. The amount of long-wave radiation emitted corresponds to the temperature of the lowest levels of the cloud. (Clouds with warmer bases emit more long-wave radiation downward than colder clouds.)

CONDUCTION AND CONVECTION

Energy that is not radiated away from Earth is either absorbed or scattered by the atmosphere or absorbed by the surface of Earth. The land surface of Earth is heated by conduction, where heat is transferred from one molecule or object to another by direct contact. The magnitude of heat flux by conduction below a surface depends on the thermal conductivity and the vertical gradient of temperature in the material beneath the surface. Soils such as dry peat, which has very low thermal conductivity (i.e., 0.06 watt per metre [.018 watt per foot] per K), permit little heat flux. In contrast, concrete has a thermal conductivity about 75 times as large (i.e., 4.60 watts per metre [1.4 watts per foot] per K) and allows substantial heat flux. In water, the thermal conductivity is relatively unimportant, since, in contrast to land surfaces, insolation extends to substantial depths in the water. In addition, water can be mixed vertically.

Convection (vertical mixing), or the flow of heat energy as warmer matter is replaced by cooler matter, occurs in the atmosphere as well as in bodies of water. This process of mixing is also referred to as turbulence. It is a mechanism of heat flux that occurs in the atmosphere in two forms. When the surface is substantially warmer than the overlying air, mixing will spontaneously occur in order to redistribute the heat. This process, referred to as free convection, occurs when the environmental lapse rate (the rate of change of an atmospheric variable, such as temperature or density, with increasing altitude) of temperature decreases at a rate greater than 1 °C per 100 metres (approximately 1 °F per 150 feet). This rate is called the adiabatic lapse rate (the rate of temperature change occurring within a rising or descending air parcel). In the ocean, the temperature increase with depth that results in free convection is dependent on the temperature, salinity, and depth of the water. For example, if the surface has a temperature of 20 °C (68 °F) and a salinity of 34.85 parts per thousand, an increase in temperature with depth of greater than about 0.19 °C per km (0.55 °F per mile) just below in the upper layers of the ocean will result in free convection. In the atmosphere, the temperature profile with height determines whether free convection occurs or not. In the ocean, free convection depends on the temperature and salinity profile with depth. Colder and more saline conditions in a surface parcel of water, for example, make it more likely for that parcel to sink spontaneously and thus become part of the process of free convection.

Mixing can also occur because of the shear stress of the wind on the surface. Shear stress is the pulling force of a fluid moving in one direction as it passes close to a fluid or object moving in another. As a result of surface friction, the average wind velocity at Earth's surface must be zero unless that surface is itself moving, such as in rivers or ocean currents. Winds above the surface decelerate when the vertical wind shear (the change in wind velocity at differing altitudes) becomes large enough to result in vertical mixing. The process by which heat and other atmospheric properties are mixed as a result of wind shear is called forced convection. Free and forced convection are also called convective and mechanical turbulence, respectively. This convection occurs as either sensible turbulent heat flux (heat directly transported to or from a surface) or latent turbulent heat flux (heat used to evaporate water from a surface). When this mixing does not occur, wind speeds are weak and change little with time. Plumes from power-plant stacks within this layer, for example, spread very little in the vertical and remain in close proximity to the stacks.

THE WATER BUDGET

The water budget refers to the input and output of water in Earth's atmosphere. The water budget at the air-surface interface is of crucial importance in influencing atmospheric processes. The surface gains water through precipitation (rain and snow), direct condensation, and deposition (dew and frost). On land, the precipitation is often so large that some of it infiltrates into the ground or runs off into streams, rivers, lakes, and the oceans. Some of the precipitation remaining on the surface, such as in puddles or on vegetation, immediately evaporates back into the atmosphere.

Liquid water in the soil is also converted to water vapour by transpiration from the leaves and stems of plants and by evaporation. The roots of vegetation may extract water from within the soil and emit it through stoma, or small openings, on the leaves. In addition, water may be evaporated from the surface of the soil directly, when groundwater from below is diffused upward. Evaporation occurs at the surface of water bodies at a rate that is inversely proportional to the relative humidity immediately above the surface. Evaporation is rapid in dry air but much slower when the lowest levels of the atmosphere are close to saturation. Evaporation from soils is dependent on the rate at which moisture is supplied by capillary suction within the soil, whereas transpiration from vegetation is dependent on both the water available within the root zone of plants and whether the stoma are open on the leaf surfaces. Water that evaporates and transpires into the atmosphere is often transported long distances before it precipitates out.

The input, transport, and removal of water from the atmosphere is part of the hydrologic cycle. At any one time, only a very small fraction of Earth's water is present within the atmosphere. If all the atmospheric water was condensed out, it would cover the surface of the planet only to an average of about 2.5 centimetres (1 inch).

THE NITROGEN BUDGET

The nitrogen budget, that is, the sum of all the inflows and outflows of nitrogen moving from Earth's atmosphere to the surface and back, involves the chemical

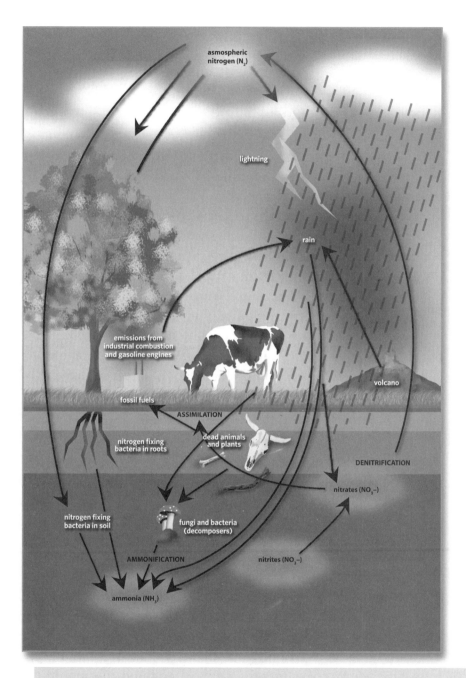

The nitrogen cycle is the process by which nitrogen is given off or absorbed on Earth. The atmosphere contains most of Earth's nitrogen (between 70 percent and 80 percent). Illustration by Tahara Anderson. © Rosen Publishing

transformation of diatomic nitrogen (N_2), which makes up 78 percent of the atmospheric gases, into compounds containing ammonium (NH^+), nitrite (NO_2^-), and nitrate (NO_3^-). In a process called nitrification, or nitrogen fixation, bacteria such as *Rhizobium* living within nodules on the roots of peas, clover, and other legumes convert diatomic nitrogen gas to ammonia. A small amount of nitrogen is also fixed by lightning. Ammonia may be further transformed by other bacteria into nitrites and nitrates and used by plants for growth. These compounds are eventually converted back to N_2 after the plants die or are eaten by denitrifying bacteria. These bacteria, in their consumption of plants and both the excrement and corpses of plant-eating animals, convert much of the nitrogen compounds back to N_2. Some of these compounds are also converted to N_2 by a series of chemical processes associated with ultraviolet light from the Sun. The combustion of petroleum by motor vehicles also produces oxides of nitrogen, which enhance the natural concentrations of these compounds. Smog, which occurs in many urban areas, is associated with substantially higher levels of nitrogen oxides.

THE SULFUR BUDGET

On Earth at any given time there is a certain amount of sulfur. The accounting of the sulfur sources and sinks, and the movement of sulfur compounds from the atmosphere to the surface and from Earth (both from rocks under and on the surface and from living things) back into the atmosphere is contained within the sulfur budget. Sulfur is put into the atmosphere as a result of weathering of sulfur-containing rocks and by intermittent volcanic emissions. Organic forms of sulfur are incorporated into living organisms and represent an important component in both the structure and the function of proteins. Sulfur also appears

The eruption of Mount St. Helens volcano, viewed here during its eruption on May 18, 1980, released sulfur into the atmosphere. Photo by Austin Post, U.S. Geological Survey

in the atmosphere as the gas sulfur dioxide (SO_2) and as part of particulate compounds containing sulfate (SO_4). Alone, both are directly dry-deposited or precipitated out onto Earth's surface. When wetted, these compounds are converted to caustic sulfuric acid (H_2SO_4).

Since the beginning of the Industrial Revolution, human activities have injected significant quantities of sulfur into the atmosphere through the combustion of fossil fuels. In and near regions of urbanization and heavy industrial activity, the enhanced deposition and precipitation of sulfur in the form of sulfuric acid, and of nitrogen oxides in the form of nitric acid (HNO_3), resulting from vehicular emissions, have been associated with damage to fish populations, forests, statues, and building exteriors. The conversion of sulfur and nitrogen oxides to acids such as H_2SO_4 and HNO_3 is commonly known as the acid rain problem. Sulfur and nitrogen oxides are precipitated in rain, snow, and dry deposition (deposition to the surface during dry weather).

THE CARBON BUDGET

The carbon budget in the atmosphere is of critical importance to climate and to life. Carbon appears in Earth's atmosphere primarily as carbon dioxide (CO_2) produced naturally by the respiration of living organisms, the decay of these organisms, the weathering of carbon-containing rock strata, and volcanic emissions. Plants utilize CO_2, water, and solar insolation to convert CO_2 to diatomic oxygen (O_2). This process, known as photosynthesis, can result in local reductions of CO_2 of tens of parts per million within vegetation canopies. In contrast, nighttime respiration occurring when photosynthesis is not active can increase CO_2 concentrations. These concentrations may even double within dense tropical forest canopies for short periods before sunrise. On the global scale, seasonal variations of about 1 percent occur as a result of CO_2 uptake from photosynthesis, plant respiration, and soil respiration. Atmospheric CO_2 is primarily absorbed in the Northern Hemisphere during the growing season (spring to autumn). CO_2 is also absorbed by ocean waters. The rate of exchange to the ocean is greater for colder than for warmer waters. Currently CO_2 makes up about 0.03 percent of the gaseous composition of the atmosphere.

In the geologic past, CO_2 levels have been significantly higher than they are today and have had a significant effect on both climate and ecology. During the Carboniferous Period (360 to 300 million years ago), for example, moderately warm and humid climates combined with high concentrations of CO_2 were associated with extensive lush vegetation. After these plants died and decomposed, they were converted to sedimentary rocks that eventually became the coal deposits currently used for industrial combustion.

In the atmosphere, certain wavelengths of long-wave radiation are absorbed and then reemitted by CO_2. Since the lower levels of the atmosphere are warmer than layers higher up, the absorption of upward-propagating electromagnetic radiation, and a reemission of a portion of it back downward, permits the lower atmosphere to remain warmer than it would be otherwise. The association of higher concentrations of CO_2 in the air with a warmer lower troposphere is commonly referred to as the greenhouse effect. (The name is inaccurate—an actual greenhouse is warmed primarily because solar radiation enters through the glass, which retains the heated air and prevents the mixing of cooler air into the greenhouse from above.) In recent years, there has been increasing concern that the release of CO_2 through the burning of coal and other fossil fuels will warm the lower atmosphere, a phenomenon commonly referred to as global warming. Water vapour is a more efficient greenhouse gas than carbon dioxide. However, since H_2O is ubiquitous, occurring in its three phases (solid, liquid, and gas), and since CO_2 is also a biogeochemically active gas, global temperature changes are both explained and predicted by changes in the atmospheric concentration of CO_2.

THE VERTICAL STRUCTURE OF THE ATMOSPHERE

As detailed above, there are many factors that influence Earth's climate and weather. To gain deeper insight into the creation of violent storms and wind, the structure of the atmosphere itself must also be understood.

Earth's atmosphere is segmented into two major zones. The homosphere is the lower of the two and the location in which turbulent mixing dominates the molecular diffusion of gases. In this region, which occurs below 100 kilometres (about 60 miles) or so, the composition of the atmosphere tends to be independent of height. Above 100 kilometres (60 miles), in the zone called the heterosphere, various atmospheric gases are separated by molecular mass, with the lighter gases being concentrated in the highest layers. Above 1,000 kilometres (about 600 miles), helium and hydrogen are the dominant species. Diatomic nitrogen (N_2), a relatively heavy gas, drops off rapidly with height and exists in only trace amounts at 500 kilometres (300 miles) and above. This decrease in the concentration of heavier gases with

Earth's atmosphere, as seen from the International Space Station in 2003. Underneath a sliver of the Moon, atmospheric layers rise from the black limb of Earth (bottom) to the lightest-shaded troposphere. NASA Marshall Space Flight Center

height is largest during periods of low Sun activity, when temperatures within the heterosphere are relatively low. The transition zone, located at a height of around 100 kilometres (60 miles) between the homosphere and heterosphere, is called the turbopause.

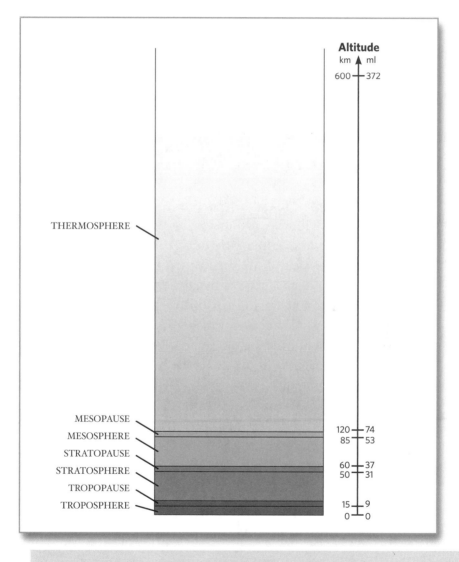

The vertical layers of Earth's atmosphere, delineated by altitude. Rosen Publishing. Adapted from NASA Education/Earth's Atmosphere

The atmosphere can be further divided into several distinct layers defined by changes in air temperature with increasing height. These layers are described below in order of increasing height above the surface.

THE TROPOSPHERE

The lowest portion of the atmosphere is the troposphere, a layer where temperature generally decreases with height. This layer contains most of Earth's clouds and is the location where weather primarily occurs.

THE PLANETARY BOUNDARY LAYER

The lower levels of the troposphere are usually strongly influenced by Earth's surface. This sublayer, known as the planetary boundary layer, is that region of the atmosphere in which the surface influences temperature, moisture, and wind velocity through the turbulent transfer of mass. As a result of surface friction, winds in the planetary boundary layer are usually weaker than above and tend to blow toward areas of low pressure. For this reason, the planetary boundary layer has also been called an Ekman layer, for Swedish oceanographer Vagn Walfrid Ekman, a pioneer in the study of the behaviour of wind-driven ocean currents.

Under clear, sunny skies over land, the planetary boundary layer tends to be relatively deep as a result of the heating of the ground by the Sun and the resultant generation of convective turbulence. During the summer, the planetary boundary layer can reach heights of 1 to 1.5 kilometres (0.6 to 1 mile) above the land surface—for example, in the humid eastern United States—and up to 5 kilometres (3 miles) in the southwestern desert. Under these conditions, when unsaturated air rises and expands, the temperature decreases at the dry adiabatic lapse rate (9.8 °C per kilometre, or roughly 23 °F per mile) throughout most of the boundary layer. Near Earth's heated surface, air temperature decreases superadiabatically (at a lapse rate greater than the dry adiabatic lapse rate). In contrast, during clear, calm nights, turbulence tends to cease, and radiational cooling (net loss of heat) from the surface results in an air temperature that increases with height above the surface.

When the rate of temperature decrease with height exceeds the adiabatic lapse rate for a region of the atmosphere, turbulence is generated. This is due to the convective overturn of the air as the warmer lower-level air rises and mixes with the cooler air aloft. In this situation, since the environmental lapse rate is greater than the adiabatic lapse rate, an ascending parcel of air remains warmer than the surrounding ambient air even though the parcel is both cooling and expanding. Evidence of this overturn is produced in the form of bubbles, or eddies, of warmer air. The larger bubbles often have sufficient buoyant energy to penetrate the top of the boundary layer. The subsequent rapid air displacement brings air from aloft into the boundary layer, thereby deepening the layer. Under these conditions of atmospheric instability, the air aloft cools according to the environmental lapse rate faster than the rising air is cooling at the adiabatic lapse rate. The air above the boundary layer replaces the rising air and undergoes compressional warming as it descends. As a result, this entrained air heats the boundary layer.

The ability of the convective bubbles to break through the top of the boundary layer depends on the environmental lapse rate aloft. The upward movement of penetrative bubbles will decrease rapidly if the parcel quickly becomes cooler than the ambient environment that surrounds it. In this situation, the air parcel will become less buoyant with additional ascent. The height that the boundary layer attains on a sunny day, therefore, is strongly influenced by the intensity of surface heating and the environmental lapse rate just above the boundary layer. The more rapidly a rising turbulent bubble cools above the boundary layer relative to the surrounding air, the lower the chance that subsequent turbulent bubbles will penetrate far above the boundary layer. The top of the daytime boundary layer is referred to as the mixed-layer inversion.

On clear, calm nights, radiational cooling results in a temperature increase with height. In this situation, known as a nocturnal inversion, turbulence is suppressed by the strong thermal stratification. Thermally stable conditions occur when warmer air overlies cooler, denser air. Over flat terrain, a nearly laminar wind flow (a pattern where winds from an upper layer easily slide past winds from a lower layer) can result. The depth of the radiationally cooled layer of air depends on a variety of factors, such as the moisture content of the air, soil and vegetation characteristics, and terrain configuration. In a desert environment, for instance, the nocturnal inversion tends to be found at greater heights than in a more humid environment. The inversion in more humid environments occurs at a lower altitude because more long-wave radiation emitted by the surface is absorbed by numerous available water molecules and reemitted back toward the surface. As a result, the lower levels of the troposphere are prevented from cooling rapidly. If the air is moist and sufficient near-surface cooling occurs, water vapour will condense into what is called "radiation fog."

Cloud Formation Within the Troposphere

The region above the planetary boundary layer is commonly known as the free atmosphere. Winds at this volume are not directly retarded by surface friction. Clouds occur most frequently in this portion of the troposphere, though fog and clouds that impinge upon or develop over elevated terrain often occur at lower levels.

There are two basic types of clouds: cumuliform and stratiform. Both cloud types develop when clear air ascends, cooling adiabatically as it expands until either water begins to condense or deposition occurs. Water undergoes a change of state from gas to liquid under these conditions, because cooler air can hold less water vapour than warmer air. For example, air at 20 °C (68 °F) can contain almost four times as much water vapour as at 0 °C (32 °F) before saturation takes place and water vapour condenses into liquid droplets.

Stratiform clouds occur as saturated air is mechanically forced upward and remains colder than the surrounding clear air at the same height. In the lower troposphere, such clouds are called stratus. Advection fog is a stratus cloud with a base lying at Earth's surface. In the middle troposphere, stratiform clouds are known as altostratus. In the upper troposphere, the terms *cirrostratus* and *cirrus* are used. The cirrus cloud type refers to thin, often wispy, cirrostratus clouds. Stratiform clouds that both extend through a large fraction of the troposphere and precipitate are called nimbostratus.

Cumuliform clouds occur when saturated air is turbulent. Such clouds, with their bubbly turreted shapes, exhibit the small-scale up-and-down behaviour of air in the turbulent planetary boundary layer. Often such clouds are seen with bases at or near the top of the boundary layer

Cirrus fibratus are high clouds that are nearly straight or irregularly curved. They appear as fine white filaments and are generally distinct from one another. Nick Impenna

as turbulent eddies generated near Earth's surface reach high enough for condensation to occur.

Cumuliform clouds will form in the free atmosphere if a parcel of air, upon saturation, is warmer than the surrounding ambient atmosphere. Since this air parcel is warmer than its surroundings, it will accelerate upward,

Altocumulus radiatus, a cloud layer with laminae arranged in parallel bands.
Lawrence Smith/Photo Researchers

creating the saturated turbulent bubble characteristic of a cumuliform cloud. Cumuliform clouds, which reach no higher than the lower troposphere, are known as cumulus humulus when they are randomly distributed and as stratocumulus when they are organized into lines. Cumulus congestus clouds extend into the middle troposphere, while deep, precipitating cumuliform clouds that extend throughout the troposphere are called cumulonimbus. Cumulonimbus clouds are also called thunderstorms, since they usually have lightning and thunder associated with them. Cumulonimbus clouds develop from cumulus humulus and cumulus congestus clouds.

Vagn Walfrid Ekman

(b. May 3, 1874, Stockholm, Swed.—d. March 9,
1954, Gostad, near Stockaryd, Swed.)

Vagn Walfrid Ekman was a Swedish physical oceanographer best known for his studies of the dynamics of ocean currents. The common oceanographic terms Ekman layer, denoting certain oceanic or atmospheric layers occurring at various interfaces; Ekman spiral, used in connection with vertical oceanic velocity; and Ekman transport, denoting wind-driven currents, derive from his research.

Ekman was the youngest son of Fredrik Laurentz Ekman, a Swedish physical oceanographer. After finishing secondary school in Stockholm, Ekman studied at the University of Uppsala, where he majored in physics. But lectures on hydrodynamics in 1897 by Vilhelm Bjerknes, one of the founders of meteorology and oceanography, definitely decided the direction of Ekman's work.

While still a student at Uppsala, Ekman made important contributions to oceanography. When it was observed, during the Norwegian North Polar Expedition, that drift ice did not follow the wind direction but deviated by 20° to 40°, Bjerknes chose Ekman to make a theoretical study of the problem. In his report, published in 1902, Ekman took into account the balance of the frictions between the wind and sea surface, within layers of water, and the deflecting force due to the Earth's rotation (Coriolis force).

After taking his degree at Uppsala in 1902, he joined the staff of the International Laboratory for Oceanographic Research in Oslo, where he remained until 1909. During those years he proved to be a skilled inventor and experimentalist. The Ekman current meter, an instrument with a simple and reliable mechanism, has been used, with subsequent improvements, to the present, while the Ekman reversing water bottle is used in freshwater lakes and sometimes in the ocean to obtain water samples at different depths with a simultaneous measurement of water temperatures.

He displayed his theoretical and experimental talents in his study of so-called dead water, which causes slow-moving boats to become stuck because of a thin layer of nearly fresh water spreading over the sea from melting ice. This phenomenon, frequently occurring in fjords, seriously impeded the Norwegian explorer Fridtjof Nansen in Arctic waters. Ekman demonstrated by experiments in a wave tank that the resistance to the motion of the vessels is increased by the waves that are formed at the interface between layers of water of different densities.

He also derived an empirical formula for the mean compressibility (compression ratio divided by pressure) of seawater as a function of pressure and temperature. This formula is still in use today to determine density of deep seawater which is compressed by hydrostatic pressure.

From 1910 to 1939, Ekman was professor of mechanics and mathematical physics at the University of Lund in Sweden, where he pursued his main interest, the dynamics of ocean currents. He published theories on wind-driven ocean currents, including the effects of coasts and bottom topography, and on the dynamics of the Gulf Stream. He also tried, with partial success, to solve the complex problem of ocean turbulence.

In 1925 Ekman participated in a cruise of a German research ship to the Canary Islands. On finding that data on currents obtained for several days at several marine stations between the Bay of Biscay and the Canary Islands were not sufficient to obtain an average figure, he and a colleague, during the years 1922–29, improved the technique for measuring currents for a prolonged period by collecting data from an anchored ship. After several preparatory cruises for that purpose off the Norwegian coast aboard a Norwegian research vessel, they made a cruise to the trade-wind region off northwestern Africa in the summer of 1930 to determine the average current at various ocean depths at stations occupied for two weeks or longer. Preliminary reports were published soon after the cruise, but Ekman wrote the final report in 1953 at the age of 79. The long delay in publication, partly owing to the loss of important data during the German occupation of Norway, also indicates the unparalleled care he took with his work.

Although his name and achievements were well known among oceanographers, he rarely attended international meetings—but his genuine kindliness prevented him from becoming a recluse. Most of his teachers and friends, such as Nansen and Bjerknes, were Norwegian. He spent many vacations in Bergen. He sang a beautiful bass, spent much time at the piano, and occasionally composed music. In the fall of 1953, he began a study of turbid currents, which he continued until a few days before his death.

The Stratosphere and Mesosphere

The stratosphere is located above the troposphere and extends up to about 50 kilometres (30 miles). Above the tropopause and the isothermal layer in the lower stratosphere, temperature increases with height. Temperatures as high as 0 °C (32 °F) are observed near the top of the stratosphere. The observed increase of temperature with height in the stratosphere results in strong thermodynamic stability with little turbulence and vertical mixing. The warm temperatures and very dry air result in an almost cloud-free volume. The infrequent clouds that do occur are called nacreous, or mother-of-pearl, clouds because of their striking iridescence, and they appear to be composed of both ice and supercooled water. These clouds form up to heights of 30 kilometres (19 miles).

The pattern of temperature increase with height in the stratosphere is the result of solar heating as ultraviolet radiation in the wavelength range of 0.200 to 0.242 micrometre dissociates diatomic oxygen (O_2). The resultant attachment of single oxygen atoms to O_2 produces ozone (O_3). Natural stratospheric ozone is produced mainly in the tropical and middle latitudes. Regions of nearly complete ozone depletion, which have occurred in the Antarctic during the spring, are associated with nacreous clouds, chlorofluorocarbons (CFCs), and other pollutants from human activities. These regions are more commonly known as ozone holes. Ozone is also transported downward into the troposphere, primarily in the vicinity of the polar front.

The stratopause caps the top of the stratosphere, separating it from the mesosphere near 45–50 kilometres (28–31 miles) in altitude and a pressure of 1 millibar (approximately equal to 0.75 mm of mercury at 0 °C, or 0.03 inch of mercury at 32 °F). In the mesosphere, temperatures again decrease with increasing altitude. Unlike the situation in the stratosphere, vertical air currents in the mesosphere are not strongly inhibited. Ice crystal clouds, called noctilucent clouds, occasionally form in the upper mesosphere. Above the mesopause, a region occurring at altitudes near 85 to 90 kilometres (50 to 55 miles), temperature again increases with height in a layer called the thermosphere.

THE THERMOSPHERE

Temperatures in the thermosphere range from near 500 K (approximately 227 °C, or 440 °F) during periods of low sunspot activity to 2,000 K (1,725 °C, or 3,137 °F) when the Sun is active. The thermopause, defined as the level of transition to a more or less isothermal temperature profile at the top of the thermosphere, occurs at heights of around 250 kilometres (150 miles) during quiet Sun periods and almost 500 kilometres (300 miles) when the Sun is active. Above 500 kilometres, molecular collisions are infrequent enough that temperature is difficult to define.

The portion of the thermosphere where charged particles (ions) are abundant is called the ionosphere. These ions result from the removal of electrons from atmospheric gases by solar ultraviolet radiation. Extending from about 80 to 300 kilometres (about 50 to 185 miles) in altitude, the ionosphere is an electrically conducting region capable of reflecting radio signals back to Earth.

Maximum ion density, a condition that makes for efficient radio transmission, occurs within two sublayers: the lower E region, which exists from 90 to 120 kilometres (about 55 to 75 miles) in altitude; and the F region, which exists from 150 to 300 kilometres (about 90 to 185 miles) in altitude. The F region has two maxima (i.e., two periods of highest ion density) during daylight hours, called F1 and F2. Both the F1 and F2 regions possess high ion density and are strongly influenced by both solar activity and time of day. Of these, the F2 region is the more variable of the two and may reach an ion density as high as 106 electrons per cubic centimetre (.06 cubic inch). Shortwave radio transmissions, capable of reaching around the world, take advantage of the ability of layers in the ionosphere to reflect certain wavelengths of electromagnetic radiation. In addition, electrical discharges from the tops of thunderstorms into the ionosphere, called transient luminous events, have been observed.

The Magnetosphere and Exosphere

Above approximately 500 kilometres (300 miles), the motion of ions is strongly constrained by the presence of Earth's magnetic field. This region of Earth's atmosphere, called the magnetosphere, is compressed by the solar wind on the daylight side of the planet and stretched outward in a long tail on the night side. The colourful auroral displays often seen in polar latitudes are associated with bursts of high-energy particles generated by the Sun. When these particles are influenced by the magnetosphere, some are subsequently injected into the lower ionosphere.

The layer above 500 kilometres is referred to as the exosphere, a region in which at least half of the upward-moving molecules do not collide with one another. In contrast, these molecules follow long ballistic trajectories and may exit the atmosphere completely if their escape velocities are high enough. The loss rate of molecules through the exosphere is critical in determining whether Earth or any other planetary body retains an atmosphere.

THE HORIZONTAL STRUCTURE OF THE ATMOSPHERE

Owing to heating and moisture differences between land and water, as well as differences in topography, Earth's atmosphere is not uniform. Just above the planet's surface, pockets of air and water vapour emerge with unique temperature and moisture characteristics. These elements contribute to the horizontal structure to the atmosphere.

THE DISTRIBUTION OF HEAT FROM THE SUN

The primary driving force for the horizontal structure of Earth's atmosphere is the amount and distribution of solar radiation that comes in contact with the planet. Earth's orbit around the Sun is an ellipse, with a perihelion (closest approach) of 147.5 million kilometres (91.7 million miles) in early January and an aphelion (farthest distance) of 152.6 million kilometres (94.8 million miles) in early July. As a result of Earth's elliptical orbit, the time between the autumnal equinox and the following vernal equinox (about September 22 to about March 21) is almost one week shorter than the remainder of the year in the Northern Hemisphere. This results in a shorter astronomical winter in the Northern Hemisphere than in the Southern Hemisphere.

Earth rotates once every 24 hours around an axis that is tilted at an angle of 23°30′ with respect to the plane of its orbit around the Sun. As a result of this tilt, during the summer season of either the Northern or the Southern Hemisphere, the Sun's rays are more direct at a given latitude than they are during the winter season. Poleward of latitudes 66°30′ N and 66°30′ S, the tilt of the planet is such that for at least one complete day (at 66°30′) and as long as six months (at 90°), the Sun is above the horizon during the summer season and below the horizon during the winter.

As a result of this asymmetric distribution of solar heating, during the winter season the troposphere in the high latitudes becomes very cold. In contrast, during the summer at high latitudes, the troposphere warms significantly as a result of the long hours of daylight. However, owing to the oblique angle of the sunlight near the poles, the temperatures there remain relatively cool compared with middle latitudes. Equatorward of latitudes 30° N and 30° S or so, substantial radiant heating from the Sun occurs during both winter and summer seasons. The tropical troposphere, therefore, has comparatively little variation in temperature during the year.

CONVECTION, CIRCULATION, AND DEFLECTION OF AIR

The region of greatest solar heating at the surface in the humid tropics corresponds to areas of deep cumulonimbus convection. Cumulonimbus clouds routinely form in the tropics where rising parcels of air are warmer than the surrounding ambient atmosphere. They transport water vapour, sensible heat, and Earth's rotational momentum to the upper portion of the troposphere. As a result of the vigorous convective mixing of the atmosphere, the tropopause in the lower latitudes is often very high, located some 17 to 18 kilometres (10.5 to 11 miles) above the surface.

Since motion upward into the stratosphere is inhibited by very stable thermal layering, the air transported upward by convection diverges toward the poles in the upper troposphere. (This divergence aloft results in a wide strip of low atmospheric pressure at the surface in the tropics, occurring in an area called the equatorial trough). As the diverted air in the troposphere moves toward the poles, it tends to retain the angular momentum of the near-equatorial region, which is large as a result of Earth's rotation. As a result, the poleward-moving air is deflected toward the right in the Northern Hemisphere and toward the left in the Southern Hemisphere.

Upon reaching around 30° of latitude poleward of its region of origin, the upper-level air is traveling primarily toward the poles and is tending toward the east. Since motion upward is constrained by the stratosphere, the slowly cooling air must descend. The compressional warming that occurs as the air descends creates vast regions of subtropical high pressure. These regions are centred over the oceans and are characterized by strong thermodynamic stability. The sparse precipitation in these regions, a result of stability and subsidence, is associated with such great arid regions of the world as the Sahara, Atacama, Kalahari, and Sonoran deserts. The accumulation of air as a result of the convergence in the upper troposphere causes deep high-pressure systems, known as subtropical ridges, to form in these regions. Locally, these ridges are given such names as the Bermuda High, the Azores High, and the North Pacific High.

The descending air referred to above, upon reaching the lower troposphere, is forced to diverge by the presence of Earth's surface. Some air moves poleward, while the remainder moves equatorward. In either direction, the air is deflected to the right in the Northern Hemisphere and to the left in the Southern Hemisphere. Deflection occurs because, in accordance with Newton's first law of motion, a parcel moving in a certain direction will retain the same motion unless acted on by an exterior force. With respect to a rotating Earth, a moving parcel conserving its momentum (i.e., not acted on by an exterior force) will appear to be deflected with respect to fixed points on the rotating Earth. As seen from a fixed point in space, such a parcel would be moving in a straight line. This apparent force on the motion of a fluid (in this case, air) is called the Coriolis effect. As a result of the Coriolis effect, air tends to rotate counterclockwise around large-scale low-pressure systems and clockwise around large-scale high-pressure systems in the Northern Hemisphere. In the Southern Hemisphere, the flow direction is reversed.

In the equatorward-moving flow, this deflection results in northeast winds north of 0° latitude and southeast winds south of that latitude. These low-level winds have been called the trade winds since 17th-century sailing vessels used them to travel to the Americas. The convergence region for lower-level northeast and southeast trade winds is called the intertropical convergence zone (ITCZ). The ITCZ corresponds to the equatorial trough and is the mechanism that helps generate the deep cumulonimbus clouds through convection. Cumulonimbus clouds are the main conduit transporting tropical heating into the upper troposphere.

The circulation pattern described above—ascent in the equatorial trough, poleward movement in the upper troposphere, descent in the subtropical ridges, and equatorward movement in the trade winds—is in effect a direct heat engine, which meteorologists call the Hadley cell. This persistent circulation mechanism transports heat from the latitudes of greatest solar insolation to the latitudes of the subtropical ridges. The geographic location of the Hadley circulation moves north and south with the seasons; however, the equatorial trough lags behind for about two months owing to the thermal inertia of Earth's surface. (For a given location on Earth's surface, the highest daily temperatures are achieved just after the period of greatest insolation, since time is required to heat the ocean surface waters and the soil.)

POLAR FRONTS AND THE JET STREAM

In the troposphere, the demarcation between polar air and warmer tropical atmosphere is usually defined by the polar front. On the poleward side of the front, the air is cold and more dense. Equatorward of the front, the air is warmer and more buoyant. During the winter season, the polar front is generally located at lower latitudes and is more pronounced than in the summer.

Cold fronts occur at the leading edge of equatorward-moving polar air. In contrast, warm fronts are well defined at the equatorward surface position of polar air as it retreats on the eastern sides of extratropical cyclones. Equatorward-moving air behind a cold front occurs in pools of dense high pressure known as polar highs and arctic highs. The term *arctic high* is used to define air that originates even deeper within the high latitudes than polar highs.

When polar air neither retreats nor advances, the polar front is called a stationary front. In the occluded stage of the life cycle of an extratropical cyclone, when cold air west of the surface low-pressure centre advances more rapidly toward the east than cold air ahead of the warm front, warmer, less-dense air is forced aloft. This frontal intersection is called an occluded front. Without exception, fronts of all types follow the movement of colder air.

Clouds and often precipitation occur on the poleward sides of both warm and stationary fronts and whenever tropical air reaching the latitude of the polar front is forced upward over the colder air near the surface. Such fronts are defined as active fronts. Rain and snowfall from active fronts form a major part of the precipitation received in the middle and high latitudes. Precipitation in these areas occurs primarily during the winter months.

The position of the polar front slopes upward toward colder air. This occurs because cold air tends to undercut the warmer air of tropical origin. Since cold air is more dense, atmospheric pressure decreases more rapidly with height on the poleward side of the polar front than on the warmer tropical side. This creates a large horizontal temperature contrast, which is essentially a large pressure gradient, between the polar and tropical air. In the middle and upper parts of the troposphere, this pressure gradient is responsible for the strong westerly winds occurring there. Winds created aloft circulate around a large region of upper-level low pressure near each of the poles. The centre of each low pressure region is a persistent cyclone known as the circumpolar vortex.

The region of strongest winds, which occurs at the juncture of the tropical and polar air masses, is called the jet stream. Since the temperature contrast between the tropics and the high latitudes is greatest in the winter, the jet stream is stronger during that season. In addition, since the mid-latitudes also become colder during the winter, while tropical temperatures remain relatively unchanged, the westerly jet stream approaches latitudes of 30° during the colder season. During the warmer season in both hemispheres, the jet stream moves poleward and is located between latitudes of 50° and 60°.

The jet stream reaches its greatest velocity at the tropopause. Above that level, a reversal of the horizontal temperature gradient occurs, which produces a reduction in the wind speeds of the jet stream at high latitudes. This causes a weakening of the westerlies with increasing height. At intervals ranging from 20 to 40 months, with a mean value of 26 months, westerly winds in the stratosphere reverse direction over low latitudes, so that an easterly flow develops. This feature is called the quasi-biennial oscillation (QBO). In addition, a phenomenon called sudden stratospheric warming, apparently the result of strong downward air motion, also occurs in the late winter and spring at high latitudes. Sudden stratospheric warming can significantly alter temperature-dependent chemical reactions of ozone and other reactive gases in the stratosphere and affect the development of such features as "ozone holes."

A major focus of weather forecasting in the middle and high latitudes is to forecast the movement and development of extratropical cyclones, polar and arctic highs, and the location and intensity of subtropical ridges. Spring and fall frosts, for example, are associated with the equatorward movement of polar highs behind a cold front, while droughts and heat waves in the summer are associated with unusually strong subtropical ridges.

Rossby Waves

Rossby waves are large horizontal atmospheric undulations associated with the polar-front jet stream and separates cold, polar air from warm, tropical air. These waves are named for Carl-Gustaf Arvid Rossby, who first identified them and explained their movement.

Rossby waves are formed when polar air moves toward the Equator, while tropical air is moving poleward. Because of the temperature difference between the Equator and the poles due to differences in the amounts of solar radiation received, heat tends to flow from low to high latitudes. This is accomplished, in part, by these air movements. Rossby waves are a dominant component of the Ferrel circulation. The tropical air carries heat poleward, and the polar air absorbs heat as it moves toward the Equator. The existence of these waves explains the low-pressure cells (cyclones) and high-pressure cells (anticyclones) that are important in producing the weather of the middle and higher latitudes.

THE EFFECTS OF THE CONTINENTS ON AIR MOVEMENT

Preferred geographic locations exist for subtropical ridges and for the development, movement, and decay of extra-tropical cyclones. During the winter months in middle and high latitudes, the lower parts of the troposphere over continents often serve as reservoirs of cold air as heat is radiated into space throughout the long nights. In contrast, the oceans lose heat less rapidly, because of the large heat capacity of water, their ability to overturn as the surfaces cool and become negatively buoyant, and the movement of ocean currents such as the Gulf Stream and the Kuroshio current. Warm currents transport heat from lower latitudes poleward and tend to occur on the western sides of oceans. The lower troposphere over these warmer oceanic areas tends to be a region of relative low pressure. As a result of this juxtaposition of cold air and warm air, the eastern sides of continents and the western fringes of oceans in middle and high latitudes are the preferred locations for extratropical storm development. Over Asia in particular, the cold high-pressure system is sufficiently permanent that a persistent offshore flow called the winter monsoon occurs.

An inverse type of flow develops in the summer as the continents heat more rapidly than their adjacent oceanic areas. Continental areas tend to become regions of relative low pressure, while high pressure in the lower troposphere becomes more prevalent offshore. As the winds travel from areas of higher pressure to areas of lower pressure, a persistent onshore flow develops over large landmasses in the lower troposphere. The result of this heating is referred to as the summer monsoon. The leading edge of this monsoon is associated with a feature called the monsoon trough, a region of low atmospheric pressure at sea level. Tropical moisture carried onshore by the summer monsoon often results in copious rainfall. The village of Cherrapunji in northeastern India, for instance, recorded over 9 metres (about 30 feet) of rain in one month (July 1861) owing to the Indian summer monsoon.

As a result of the continental effect, the subtropical ridge is segmented into surface high-pressure cells. In the summer, large landmasses in the subtropics tend to be centres of relative low pressure as a result of strong solar heating. As a consequence, persistent high-pressure cells, such as the Bermuda and Azores highs, occur over the oceans. The oval shape of these high-pressure cells creates a thermal structure on their eastern sides that differs from the thermal structure on their western sides in the lower troposphere. On the eastern side, subsidence from the Hadley circulation is enhanced by the tendency of air to preserve its angular momentum on the rotating Earth. Owing to the enhanced descent of air over the eastern parts of the oceans, landmasses adjacent to these areas (typically the western sides of continents) tend to be deserts, such as those found in northwestern and southwestern Africa and along western coastal Mexico.

THE EFFECTS OF THE OCEANS ON AIR MOVEMENT

The arid conditions found along the western coasts of continents in subtropical latitudes are further enhanced by the influence of the equatorward surface air flow on the ocean currents. This flow exerts a shearing stress on the ocean surface, which results in the deflection of the upper layer of water above the thermocline to the right in the Northern Hemisphere and to the left in the Southern Hemisphere. (This deflection is also the result of the Coriolis effect; water from both hemispheres moves westward when displaced toward the Equator.) As warmer surface waters are carried away by this offshore ocean airflow, cold water from below the thermocline rises to the surface in a process called upwelling. Upwelling creates areas of cold coastal surface waters that stabilize the lower troposphere and reduce the chances for convection. Lower convection in turn reduces the likelihood for precipitation, although fogs and low stratus clouds are common. Upwelling regions are also associated with enriched sea life, as oxygen and organic nutrients are transported upward from the depths toward the surface of the ocean.

During periods when the ITCZ is located near the Equator, trade winds from the northeast and southeast converge there. The westward-moving winds cause the displacement of surface ocean waters away from the Equator such that the deeper, colder waters move to the surface. In the central and eastern Pacific Ocean near the Equator, when this upwelling is stronger than average, the event is called La Niña. When the trade winds weaken in this region, however, warmer-than-average surface conditions occur, and upwelling is weaker than usual. This event is called El Niño. Changes in ocean surface temperatures caused by El Niño significantly affect where cumulonimbus clouds form in the ITCZ and, therefore, the geographic structure of the Hadley cell. During periods when El Niño is active, weather patterns across the entire Earth are substantially altered.

MOUNTAIN BARRIERS

North-south-oriented mountain barriers, such as the Rockies and the Andes, and large massifs, such as the Plateau of Tibet, also influence atmospheric flow. When the general westerly flow in the mid-latitudes reaches these barriers, air tends to be blocked. It is transported poleward west of the terrain and toward the Equator east of the obstacle. Air forced up the slopes of mountain barriers is often sufficiently moist to produce considerable precipitation on windward sides of mountains, whereas subsiding air on the lee slopes produces more-arid conditions. Essentially, the elevated terrain affects the atmosphere as if it were an anticyclone, a centre of high pressure. In addition, mountains prevent cold air from the continental interior from moving westward of the terrain. As a result, relatively mild weather occurs along the western coasts of continents with north-south mountain ranges when compared with continental interiors. For example, the West Coast of North America experiences milder winter weather than the Great Plains and Midwest, both of which occur at similar latitudes. In contrast, east-west mountain barriers, such as the Alps in Europe, offer little impediment to the general westerly flow of air. In these situations, milder maritime conditions extend much farther inland.

CLOUD FORMATION AND PROCESSES

Together, the movement of air and the positions of low and high pressure areas have a large impact on where and what kinds of clouds will develop. Cloud formation is governed by the condensation of water vapour into droplets of liquid water or ice crystals. If these products of condensation grow large enough, they fall to the ground. Water droplets and ice crystals often interact with light and one another to produce commonly observed optical phenomena.

CONDENSATION

The formation of cloud droplets and cloud ice crystals is associated with suspended aerosols, which are produced by natural processes as well as human activities and are ubiquitous in Earth's atmosphere. In the absence of such aerosols, the spontaneous conversion of water vapour into liquid water or ice crystals requires conditions with relative humidities much greater than 100 percent, with respect to a flat surface of H_2O. The development of clouds in such a fashion, which occurs only in a controlled laboratory environment, is referred to as homogeneous nucleation. Air containing water vapour with a relative humidity greater than 100 percent, with respect to a flat surface, is referred to as being supersaturated. In the atmosphere, aerosols serve as initiation sites for the condensation or deposition of water vapour. Since their surfaces are of discrete sizes, aerosols reduce the amount of supersaturation required for water vapour to change its phase and are referred to as cloud condensation nuclei.

The larger the aerosol and the greater its solubility, the lower the supersaturation percentage required for the aerosol to serve as a condensation surface. Condensation nuclei in the atmosphere become effective at supersaturations of around 0.1 to 1 percent (that is, levels of water vapour around 0.1 to 1 percent above the point of saturation). The concentration of cloud condensation nuclei in the lower troposphere at a supersaturation of 1 percent ranges from around 100 per cubic centimetre (approximately 1,600 per cubic inch) in size in oceanic air to 500 per cubic centimetre (8,000 per cubic inch) in the atmosphere over a continent. Higher concentrations occur in polluted air.

Aerosols that are effective for the conversion of water vapour to ice crystals are referred to as ice nuclei. In contrast to cloud condensation nuclei, the most effective ice nuclei are hydrophobic (having a low affinity for water) with molecular spacings and a crystallographic structure close to that of ice.

While cloud condensation nuclei are always readily available in the atmosphere, ice nuclei are often scarce. As a result, liquid water cooled below 0 °C (32 °F) can often remain liquid at subfreezing temperatures because of the absence of effective ice nuclei. Liquid water at temperatures less than 0 °C is referred to as supercooled water. Except for true ice crystals, which are effective at 0 °C, all other ice nuclei become effective at temperatures below freezing. In the absence of any ice nuclei, the freezing of supercooled water droplets of a few micrometres in radius, in a process called homogeneous ice nucleation, requires temperatures at or lower than -39 °C (-38 °F). While a raindrop will freeze near 0 °C, small cloud droplets have too few molecules to create an ice crystal by random chance until the molecular motion is slowed as the temperature approaches -39 °C. When ice nuclei are present, heterogeneous ice nucleation can occur at warmer temperatures.

Ice nuclei are of three types: deposition nuclei, contact nuclei, and freezing nuclei. Deposition nuclei are analogous to condensation nuclei in that water vapour directly deposits as ice crystals on the aerosol. Contact and freezing nuclei, in contrast, are associated with the conversion of supercooled water to ice. A contact nucleus converts liquid water to ice by touching a supercooled water droplet. Freezing nuclei are absorbed into the liquid water and convert the supercooled water to ice from the inside out.

Examples of cloud condensation nuclei include sodium chloride (NaCl) and ammonium sulfate ([NH$_4$]$_2$ SO$_2$), whereas the clay mineral kaolinite is an example of an ice nuclei. In addition, naturally occurring bacteria found in decayed leaf litter can serve as ice nuclei at temperatures of less than about -4 °C (24.8 °F). In a process called cloud seeding, silver iodide, with effective ice-nucleating temperatures of less than -4 °C, has been used for years in attempts to convert supercooled water to ice crystals in regions with a scarcity of natural ice nuclei.

PRECIPITATION

The evolution of clouds that follows the formation of liquid cloud droplets or ice crystals depends on which phase of water occurs. A cloud in which only liquid water occurs (even at temperatures less than 0 °C) is referred to as a warm cloud, and the precipitation that results is said to be due to warm-cloud processes. In such a cloud, the growth of a liquid water droplet to a raindrop begins with condensation, as additional water vapour condenses in a supersaturated atmosphere. This process continues until the droplet has attained a radius of about 10 micrometres (0.0004 inch). Above this size, since the mass of the droplet increases according to the cube of its radius, further increases by condensational growth are very slow. Subsequent growth, therefore, occurs only when the cloud droplets develop at slightly different rates. Differences in growth rates have been attributed to differences in spatial variations of the initial aerosol sizes, in solubilities, and in magnitudes of supersaturation. Cloud droplets of different sizes will fall at different velocities and will collide with droplets of different radii. If the collision is hard enough to overcome the surface tension between the two colliding droplets, coalescence will occur and result in a new and larger single droplet.

This process of cloud-droplet growth is referred to as collision-coalescence. Warm-cloud rain results when the droplets attain a sufficient size to fall to the ground. Such a raindrop (perhaps about 1 mm [0.04 inch] in radius) contains perhaps one million 10-micrometre cloud droplets. The typical radii of raindrops resulting from this type of precipitation process range up to several millimetres and have fall velocities of around 3 to 4 metres (10 to 13 feet) per second. This type of precipitation is very common from shallow cumulus clouds over tropical oceans. In these locations, the concentration of cloud condensation nuclei is so small that there is only limited competition for the available water vapour.

THE PRECIPITATION OF ICE

A cloud that contains ice crystals is referred to as a cold cloud, and the resulting precipitation is said to be the product of cold-cloud processes. Traditionally, this process has also been referred to as the Bergeron-Findeisen mechanism, for Swedish meteorologists Tor Bergeron and Walter Findeisen, who introduced it in the 1930s. In this type of cloud, ice crystals can grow directly from the deposition of water vapour. This water vapour may be supersaturated with respect to ice, or it may be the result of evaporation of supercooled water and subsequent deposition onto an ice crystal. Since the saturation vapour pressure of liquid water is always greater than or equal to the saturation vapour pressure of ice, ice crystals will grow at the expense of the liquid water. For example, saturated air with respect to liquid water becomes super-saturated with respect to ice by 10 percent at -10 °C (14 °F) and by 21 percent at -20 °C (-4 °F). This results in a rapid conversion of liquid water to ice. This substantial and rapid change of phase permits large ice crystals in a cloud surrounded by a large number of supercooled cloud droplets to grow quickly (often in less than 15 minutes) from tiny ice crystals to snowflakes. These snowflakes are large enough to fall by depositional growth alone. Fall velocities of snow range up to about 2 metres per second (6.5 feet per second). Ice crystals that grow by deposition have much lower densities than solid ice because of the air pockets occurring within the volume of the crystal. This lower density differentiates snow from ice. Clouds that are completely converted to ice crystals are referred to as glaciated clouds.

The specific form the ice crystals take depends on the temperature and the degree of supersaturation with respect to ice. At -14 °C (7 °F) and a relatively large supersaturation with respect to liquid water, for example, ice crystals with dendritic (treelike branching) patterns form. This type of ice crystal, the one usually used to represent snowflakes in photographs and drawings, experiences growth at the end of radial arms on one or more planes of

The crystalline structure of a snowflake, as viewed under a microscope. Ice crystals are the result of supercooling of water droplets in clouds. De Agostini Picture Library/Getty Images

the crystal. At -40 °C (-40 °F) and a supersaturation with respect to liquid water of close to 0 percent, hollow ice columns form.

Ice crystals can also grow large enough to precipitate either by aggregation or by riming. Aggregation occurs when the arms of the ice crystals interlock and form a clump. This collection of intermingled ice crystals can occasionally reach several centimetres in diameter. Ice crystals can also grow when supercooled water freezes directly onto the crystal to form rime. With greater accumulation of dense ice on the crystal, its fall velocity increases. When the riming is substantial enough, the crystal form of the snowflake is lost and replaced by a more or less spherical particle called graupel. Smaller-sized graupels are generally referred to as snow grains. In cumulonimbus clouds during conditions where graupels are repeatedly wetted and then injected back toward high altitudes by strong updrafts, very large graupels called hail result. Hail has been observed on the ground at sizes larger than grapefruits.

Frozen precipitation, falling to levels of the atmosphere that are much warmer than 0 °C (32 °F), often melts and reaches the ground as rain. Such cold-cloud rain at the ground is usually distinguished from warm-cloud rain by its larger size. Melted hailstones, in particular, make a large-radius impact when they strike the ground. Cold-cloud rain occasionally will refreeze if a layer of subfreezing air exists near Earth's surface. When this freezing occurs in the free atmosphere, the frozen raindrops are referred to as sleet or ice pellets. When this freezing occurs only upon the impact of the raindrop with the ground, the precipitation is known as freezing rain. During ice storms, freezing rain can produce accumulations heavy enough to snap large trees and electrical lines.

LIGHTNING AND OPTICAL PHENOMENA

The repeated collision of ice crystals and graupel in clouds is associated with the buildup of electrical charge. This electrification is particularly large in cumulonimbus clouds as a result of vigorous vertical mixing and collisions. On average, positive charges accumulate in the upper regions, while negative charges are concentrated lower down. In response to the negative charge near the cloud base, and as negatively charged rain falls toward the ground, a pocket of positive charge develops on the ground. When the difference in electric potential between positive and negative charges becomes large enough, a sudden electrical discharge (lightning) will occur. Lightning can occur between different regions of

Cloud Research

The presence of cloud condensation and ice nuclei in air parcels is tested by using cloud chambers in which controlled temperatures and relative humidities are specified. In the upper troposphere and lower stratosphere, aircraft fly through clouds collecting droplets and ice on collection plates or photographing their presence in the airstream. In the past, identification of the different sizes of droplets and of the various types of ice crystals was performed by a researcher in a tedious and subjective procedure. Today this analysis can be automated by computerized image assessment. On the ground, rainfall impaction molds and snow crystal impressions are made. Hailstones are also collected, since an analysis of their structure often helps define the ambient environment in which they formed. Chemical analyses of the cloud droplets, ice crystals, and precipitation are also frequently performed in order to identify natural and human-made pollutants within the different forms of water.

the cloud, as in intracloud lightning, and between the cloud and the positively charged ground, as in cloud-to-ground lightning. The passage of the lightning through the air heats it to above 30,000 K (29,725 °C, or 53,540 °F), causing a large increase in pressure. This produces a powerful shock wave that is heard as thunder.

Sunlight that propagates through clouds and precipitation often produces fascinating optical images. Rainbows are produced when sunlight is diffracted into its component colours by water droplets. In addition, halos are produced by the refraction and reflection of sunlight or moonlight by ice crystals, while coronas are formed when sunlight or moonlight passes through water droplets.

Chapter 2

WINDS AND WINDSTORMS

Winds play a significant role in determining and controlling climate and weather. They occur as global and regional phenomena driven by the heating differences between land and water or restricted phenomena with strong ties to local topography. They occur just above the surface or at high altitudes and move pockets of air from one area to another. In some parts of the world at certain times of the year, the interaction between Earth's surface and the winds traveling above it spawn destructive cyclones.

WIND

In climatology, wind can be defined as the movement of air relative to the surface of the Earth. Wind occurs because of horizontal and vertical differences (gradients) in atmospheric pressure. Accordingly, the distribution of winds is closely related to that of pressure. Near the Earth's surface, winds generally flow around regions of relatively low and high pressure—cyclones and anticyclones, respectively. They rotate counterclockwise around lows in the Northern Hemisphere and clockwise around those in the Southern Hemisphere. Similarly, wind systems rotate around the centres of highs in the opposite direction.

In the middle and upper troposphere, the pressure systems are organized in a sequence of high-pressure ridges and low-pressure troughs, rather than in the closed, roughly circular systems nearer the surface of the Earth. They have a wavelike motion and interact to form a rather complex series of ridges and troughs. The largest of the wave patterns are the so-called standing waves that have three or four ridges and a corresponding number of troughs in a broad band in middle latitudes of the Northern Hemisphere. The westerlies of the Southern Hemisphere are much less strongly affected by standing disturbances. Associated with these long standing waves are the short waves (several hundred kilometres in wavelength) called traveling waves. Such traveling waves form the upper parts of near-surface cyclones and anticyclones to which they are linked, thus guiding their movement and development.

At high latitudes the winds are generally easterly near the ground. In low, tropical, and equatorial latitudes, the northeasterly trade winds north of the intertropical convergence zone (ICZ), or thermal equator, and the southeasterly trade winds south of the ICZ move toward the ICZ, which migrates north and south with the seasonal position of the Sun. Vertically, winds then rise and create towering cumulonimbus clouds and heavy rain on either side of the ICZ, which marks a narrow belt of near calms known as the doldrums. The winds then move poleward near the top of the troposphere before sinking again in the subtropical belts in each hemisphere. From here, winds again move toward the Equator as trade winds. These gigantic cells with overturning air in each of the hemispheres in low latitudes are known as the Hadley cells. In the mid-latitudes, oppositely rotating wind systems called Ferrel cells carry surface air poleward and upper tropospheric air toward the Hadley cells. The three-dimensional pattern of winds over the Earth, known as general circulation, is responsible for the fundamental latitudinal structure of pressure and air movement and, hence, of climates.

On a smaller scale are the local winds, systems that are associated with specific geographic locations and reflect the influence of topographic features. The most common of these local wind systems are the sea and land breezes, mountain and valley breezes, foehn winds (also called chinook, or Santa Ana, winds), and katabatic winds. Local winds exert a pronounced influence on local climate and are themselves affected by local weather conditions.

Wind speeds and gustiness are generally strongest by day when the heating of the ground by the Sun causes overturning of the air, the descending currents conserving the angular momentum of high-altitude winds. By night, the gustiness dies down and winds are generally lighter.

THE BEAUFORT SCALE

Throughout time, people have noticed the effects of the wind on their surroundings. In 1805, a commander in the British Navy took these observations one step further and tried to classify the wind's force at sea. Devised by Comdr. (later Admiral and Knight Commander of the Bath) Francis Beaufort of the British Navy, the Beaufort wind force scale was originally based on the effect of the wind on a full-rigged man-of-war. In 1838 it became mandatory for log entries in all ships in the Royal Navy. Altered to include observations of the state of the sea and phenomena on land as criteria, it was adopted in 1874 by the International Meteorological Committee for international use in weather telegraphy.

The Beaufort scale as originally drawn up made no reference to the speed of the wind, and various attempts, particularly during the 20th century, have been made to correlate the two. An attempt made in 1912 by the

International Commission for Weather Telegraphers was interrupted by World War I. In 1921 G.C. Simpson was asked to formulate equivalents, which were accepted in 1926 by the Committee. In June 1939 the International Meteorological Committee adopted a table of values referring to an anemometer at a height of 6 metres (20 feet). This was not immediately adopted by the official weather services of the United States and Great Britain, which used the earlier scale referring to an anemometer at an elevation of 11 metres (36 feet). The Beaufort force numbers 13 to 17 were added by the U.S. Weather Bureau in 1955.

The scale is now rarely used by professional meteorologists, having been largely replaced by more objective methods of determining wind speeds. Nevertheless, it is still useful in estimating the wind characteristics over a large area, and it may be used to estimate the wind where there are no wind instruments. The Beaufort scale also can be used to measure and describe the effects of different wind velocities on objects on land or at sea. The terms for winds that are used by the U.S. National Weather Service sometimes differ from those used by other countries.

WIND-GENERATED TURBULENCE

During windy conditions, the mechanical production of turbulence becomes important. Turbulence eddies produced by wind shear tend to be smaller in size than the turbulence bubbles produced by the rapid convection of buoyant air. Within a few tens of metres of the surface during windy conditions, the wind speed increases dramatically with height. If the winds are sufficiently strong, the turbulence generated by wind shear can overshadow the resistance of layered, thermally stable air.

In general, there tends to be little turbulence above the boundary layer in the troposphere. Even so, there are two notable exceptions. First, turbulence is produced near jet streams, where large velocity shears exist both within and adjacent to cumuliform clouds. In these locations, buoyant turbulence occurs as a result of the release of latent heat. Second, pockets of buoyant turbulence may be found at and just above cloud tops. In these locations, the radiational cooling of the clouds destabilizes pockets of air and makes them more buoyant. Clear-air turbulence (CAT) is frequently reported when aircraft fly near one of these regions of turbulence generation.

The top of the troposphere, called the tropopause, corresponds to the level in which the pattern of decreasing temperature with height ceases. It is replaced by a layer that is essentially isothermal (of equal temperature). In the tropics and subtropics, the tropopause is high, often reaching to about 18 kilometres (11 miles), as a result of vigorous vertical mixing of the lower atmosphere by thunderstorms. In polar regions, where such deep atmospheric turbulence is much less frequent, the tropopause is often as low as 8 kilometres (5 miles). Temperatures at the tropopause range from as low as -80 °C (-112 °F) in the tropics to -50 °C (-58 °F) in polar regions.

THE NATURE OF STORMS

Storms are violent atmospheric disturbances, characterized by low barometric pressure, cloud cover, precipitation, strong winds, and possibly lightning and thunder.

Storm is a generic term, popularly used to describe a large variety of atmospheric disturbances, ranging from ordinary rain showers and snowstorms to thunderstorms, wind and wind-related disturbances, such as gales, tornadoes, tropical cyclones, and sandstorms.

Wind Shear

Wind shear is a rapid change in wind velocity or direction. A very narrow zone of abrupt velocity change is known as a shear line. Wind shear is observed both near the ground and in jet streams, where it may be associated with clear-air turbulence. Vertical wind shear that causes turbulence is closely associated with the vertical and horizontal transport of momentum, heat, and water vapour.

In meteorological terminology storm is restricted to a cyclone with a strong low pressure centre, strong winds, ranging from 103–117 kilometres per hour (64–73 miles per hour), accompanied by heavy precipitation, and at times, lightning and thunder.

CYCLONES

Any large system of winds that circulates about a centre of low atmospheric pressure in a counterclockwise direction north of the Equator and in a clockwise direction to the south is called a cyclone. Cyclonic winds move across nearly all regions of the Earth except the equatorial belt and are generally associated with rain or snow. Also occurring in much the same areas are anticyclones, wind systems that rotate about a high-pressure centre. Anticyclones are so called because they have a flow opposite to that of cyclones—i.e., an outward-spiralling motion, with the winds rotating clockwise in the Northern Hemisphere and counterclockwise in the Southern. These winds are usually not as strong as the cyclonic variety and commonly produce no precipitation.

Cyclones occur chiefly in the middle and high latitude belts of both hemispheres. In the Southern Hemisphere, where most of the terrestrial surface is covered by the oceans, cyclones are distributed in a relatively uniform manner through various longitudes. Characteristically, they form in latitudes 30° to 40° S and move in a generally southeasterly direction, reaching maturity in latitudes around 60°. The situation is quite different in the Northern Hemisphere. There, continental landmasses extend from the Equator to the Arctic, and large mountain belts interfere with the midlatitude air currents, giving rise to significant variations in the occurrence of cyclones (and anticyclones). Certain tracks are favoured by the wind systems. The principal cyclone tracks lie over the oceans,

Cyclone Catarina, as viewed from the International Space Station. It struck Brazil in late March 2004. National Aeronautics and Space Administration (NASA) (Image Number: ISS008-E-19646)

regularly traversing to the east of both mountain barriers and continental coastlines.

Cyclones that form closer to the Equator (i.e., at latitudes 10° to 25° north and south over the oceans) differ somewhat in character from the extratropical variety. Such wind systems, known as tropical cyclones, are much smaller in diameter. Whereas extratropical cyclones range from nearly 1,000 to 4,000 kilometres (620 to 2,500 miles) across, tropical cyclones typically measure only about 100 to over 1,000 kilometres (62 to 620 miles) in diameter. They also tend to be more violent than those occurring in the midlatitudes and can cause considerable damage. Their wind velocities may reach up to 90 metres per second (200 miles per hour), as opposed to a maximum of about 30 metres per second (67 miles per hour) for extratropical cyclones. In the Atlantic and Caribbean regions, tropical cyclones with winds of at least 33 metres per second (74 miles per hour) averaged over one-minute intervals are called hurricanes, while in the western Pacific and China Sea, the term typhoon is applied.

EXTRATROPICAL CYCLONES

Extratropical cyclones, or wave cyclones, are storm systems that form in regions of large horizontal temperature variations called frontal zones. They present a contrast to the more violent cyclones or hurricanes of the tropics, which form in regions of relatively uniform temperatures.

According to the polar-front theory, extratropical cyclones develop when a wave forms on a frontal surface separating a warm air mass from a cold air mass. As the amplitude of the wave increases, the pressure at the centre of disturbance falls, eventually intensifying to the point at which a cyclonic circulation begins. The decay of such a system results when the cold air from the north in the Northern Hemisphere, or from the south in the Southern Hemisphere, on the western side of such a cyclone sweeps under all of the warm tropical air of the system so that the entire cyclone is composed of the cold air mass. This action is known as occlusion.

Typical weather sequences are associated with extratropical cyclones. Stations ahead of the approaching front side of the wave, called the warm front, normally experience increasingly thickening and lowering clouds, followed by precipitation, which normally persists until the centre of the cyclone passes by the station. If the station is located far to the south of the cyclone centre, then usually only a relatively short period of precipitation occurs during the passage of the back side of the wave, called the cold front. In high and middle latitudes a number of extratropical cyclones normally exist around the globe at any given time. These storms tend to form in preferred locations and follow typical paths, although exceptions to these typical patterns often occur.

Intertropical Convergence Zone (ITCZ)

The ITCZ, or equatorial convergence zone, is a belt of converging trade winds and rising air that encircles the Earth near the Equator. The rising air produces high cloudiness, frequent thunderstorms, and heavy rainfall. The doldrums, oceanic regions of calm surface air, occur within the zone. The ITCZ shifts north and south seasonally with the Sun. Over the Indian Ocean, it undergoes especially large seasonal shifts of 40°–45° of latitude.

WINDSTORMS

A wind that is strong enough to cause at least light damage to trees and buildings and may or may not be accompanied by precipitation is called a windstorm. Wind speeds during a windstorm typically exceed 55 kilometres (34 miles) per hour. Wind damage can be attributed to gusts (short bursts of high-speed winds) or longer periods of stronger sustained winds. Although tornadoes and tropical cyclones also produce wind damage, they are usually classified separately.

Windstorms may last for just a few minutes when caused by downbursts from thunderstorms, or they may last for hours (and even several days) when they result from large-scale weather systems. A windstorm that travels in a straight line and is caused by the gust front (the boundary between descending cold air and warm air at the surface) of an approaching thunderstorm is called a derecho. Gustavus Hinrichs, a physics professor from the University of Iowa and founder of the Iowa Weather Service, applied the term *derecho*—a Spanish word that means "straight" or "right"—to straight-line winds in 1888. Derechos are capable of causing widespread damage and landscape devastation. For example, the winds of a derecho occurring in northern Minnesota, U.S., on July 4, 1999, peaked at or near 160 kilometres (100 miles) per hour and blew down tens of millions of trees.

Longer-period windstorms have two main causes: (1) large differences in atmospheric pressure across a region and (2) strong jet-stream winds overhead. Horizontal pressure differences may accelerate the surface winds substantially as air travels from a region of higher atmospheric pressure to one of lower. In addition, the vertical turbulent mixing of stronger jet-stream winds aloft can produce strong gusty winds at ground level.

Intense winter storms are frequently the cause of long-lasting windstorms. Such winter low-pressure systems have large horizontal pressure differences and are always accompanied by strong jet-stream winds aloft. In the northeastern United States, windstorms that occur as particularly strong low-pressure systems and move northward along the Atlantic Coast are called "nor'easters."

Cold fronts associated with such intense low-pressure systems can produce windstorms both as they pass and for a period afterward as colder air flows overhead. Such movement of cold air aloft is particularly effective at causing the downward mixing of jet-stream winds. Windstorms create dust storms and sandstorms in arid and semiarid regions. In North Africa, these cold frontal windstorms are often referred to as haboobs.

Blizzard conditions can occur when the windstorms pass over snow-covered ground. The U.S. National Weather Service issues blizzard warnings when sustained winds or frequent gusts are forecast to be 56 kilometres (35 miles) per hour or greater for at least three hours with sufficient blowing snow to reduce visibility to less than 400 metres (1,300 feet). This type of windstorm also produces dangerous wind chills. A wind speed of 55 kilometres (34 miles) per hour with an air temperature of $-6.5\,^{\circ}$C (20.3 $^{\circ}$F), for example, produces a loss of body heat equivalent to what occurs in calm winds with an air temperature of -29 $^{\circ}$C ($-20.2\,^{\circ}$F). When cold fronts pass over mountains, cold air accelerates even more as it moves downslope. Downslope winds are called fall winds or katabatic winds. Windstorms of this type are called boras or downslope windstorms.

Warm air flowing poleward to the east of intense low-pressure systems can also produce windstorms. In North Africa and the Arabian Peninsula such a windstorm, called khamsin, can transport large amounts of dust and sand northward. When the winds blow over mountains, the warm air is heated even further by compression as it moves toward lower altitudes. A strong, warm windstorm is called a chinook in the northwestern United States and southwestern Canada, a foehn in the European Alps, and a zonda in the Andes Mountains of Argentina. In 1972 a chinook in Boulder, Colo., U.S., produced a wind gust that briefly reached 215 kilometres (134 miles) per hour and caused extensive damage. Locations adjacent to large mountain barriers in the middle and higher latitudes are noted as being particularly vulnerable to downslope windstorms. At lower latitudes these intense low-pressure systems and the associated wind effects of a strong jet stream do not normally occur.

Satellite image of a large dust storm in the Takla Makan Desert, northwestern China. MODIS Rapid Response Team/NASA/GFSC

MONSOONS

Monsoons are major wind systems that seasonally reverse their direction—such as one that blows for approximately six months from the northeast and six months from the southwest. The most prominent monsoons occur in South Asia, Africa, Australia, and the Pacific coast of Central America. Monsoonal tendencies also are apparent along the Gulf Coast of the United States and in central Europe. However, true monsoons do not occur in those regions.

The primary cause of monsoons lies in different warming trends over land and sea, though other factors may be involved. Seasonal changes in temperature are large over land but small over ocean waters, and monsoons blow from atmospheric heat sinks (that is, cold regions with high atmospheric pressure) toward heat sources (warm regions characterized by low atmospheric pressure). Consequently, monsoon winds typically travel from sea to land in summer and from land to sea in winter. For example, the heat source involved in the Indian summer monsoon resides over the Plateau of Tibet and the eastern foothills of the Himalayas, while the heat sink occurs over the southern Indian Ocean and Madagascar, a region where relatively cloud-free air cools by emitting infrared, or "long-wave," radiation into space. Likewise, the heat source for the Australian summer monsoon resides over the area in which many meteorologists call the "Maritime Continent," a region made up of parts of Southeast Asia and the islands of Indonesia and the Philippines, while the heat sink resides over Siberia.

Most summer monsoons have a dominant westerly component and a strong tendency to ascend and produce copious rainfall, which occurs as a result of the condensation of water vapour in the rapidly rising air. The intensity and duration of these rains, however, are not uniform from year to year. Conversely, the winds of winter monsoons have a prevailing easterly component and a strong tendency to diverge, subside, and cause drought.

The poleward limits of monsoon systems are often sites of sharp changes in wind direction. In India, for example, the monsoon blows from the southwest in July and August, and north of India the winds are from the east. In northern Australia the monsoon arrives from the northwest during January-February. At the southern limit of the Australian monsoon, the winds turn easterly.

Climatic patterns reminiscent of monsoons also occur in areas outside of the prominent monsoon regions. In central Europe, where the average wind direction in summer differs some 30° to 40° from that of the Atlantic, there are monsoonal tendencies that occur not as a continuous flow but rather intermittently within frontal depressions, bringing cool, cloudy weather, rain, and thunderstorms. Some see in this climatic pattern a true monsoon, but it is obvious that it is only an "embryo monsoon" that results in weather singularities. The latitude is too high for a true monsoon to arise. In addition, the Gulf Coast of the United States is prone to climatic patterns with monsoonal tendencies. However, the seasonally consistent winds characteristic of true monsoons do not emerge.

THE INDIAN MONSOON

The most prominent of the world's monsoon systems is the one that primarily affects India and its surrounding water bodies. As stated above, it blows from the northeast during cooler months and reverses direction to blow from the southwest during the warmest months of the year. This process brings large amounts of rainfall to the region during June and July.

At the Equator the area near India is unique in that dominant or frequent westerly winds occur at the surface almost constantly throughout the year. The surface easterlies reach only to latitudes near 20° N in February, and even then they have a very strong northerly component. They soon retreat northward, and drastic changes take place in the upper-air circulation. This is a time of transition between the end of one monsoon and the beginning of the next. Late in March the high-sun season reaches the Equator and moves farther north. With it go atmospheric instability, convectional (that is, rising and turbulent) clouds, and rain. The westerly subtropical jet stream still controls the flow of air across northern India, and the surface winds are northeasterlies.

Indian commuters making their way through monsoon-flooded streets. Summer monsoons frequently bring heavy rainfall, especially in India. Narinder Nanu/AFP/Getty Images

Monsoon Onset and Early Developments

As the high-sun season (that is, the Northern Hemisphere summer) moves northward during April, India becomes particularly prone to rapid heating because the highlands to the north protect it from any incursions of cold air. There are three distinct areas of relative upper tropospheric warmth—namely, (1) above the southern Bay of Bengal, (2) above the Plateau of Tibet, and (3) across the trunks of the various peninsulas that are relatively dry during this time. These three areas combine to form a vast heat-source region. The relatively warm area above the southern Bay of Bengal occurs mostly at the 500–100-millibar level. (This atmospheric pressure region typically occurs at elevations between 5,500 and 16,100 metres [18,000 and 53,000 feet] but may vary according to changes in heating and cooling.) It does not appear at a lower level and is probably caused by the release of condensation heat (associated with the change from water vapour to liquid water) at the top of towering cumulonimbus clouds along the advancing intertropical convergence. In contrast, a heat sink appears over the southern Indian Ocean as the relatively cloud-free air cools by emitting long-wavelength radiation. Monsoon winds at the surface blow from heat sink to heat source. As a result, by May the southwest monsoon is well-established over Sri Lanka, an island off the southeastern tip of the Indian peninsula.

Also in May, the dry surface of Tibet (above 4,000 metres [13,100 feet]) absorbs and radiates heat that is readily transmitted to the air immediately above. At about 6,000 metres (19,700 feet) an anticyclonic cell arises, causing a strong easterly flow in the upper troposphere above northern India. The subtropical jet stream suddenly changes its course to the north of the anticyclonic ridge and the highlands, though it may occasionally reappear southward of them for very brief periods. This change of the upper tropospheric circulation above northern India from westerly jet to easterly flow coincides with a reversal of the vertical temperature and pressure gradients between 600 and 300 millibars. On many occasions the easterly wind aloft assumes jet force. It anticipates by a few days the "burst," or onset, of the surface southwesterly monsoon some 1,500 kilometres (900 miles) farther south, with a definite sequential relationship, although the exact cause is not known. Because of India's inverted triangular shape, the land is heated progressively as the sun moves northward. This accelerated spread of heating, combined with the general direction of heat being transported by winds, results in a greater initial monsoonal activity over the Arabian Sea (at late springtime), where a real frontal situation often occurs, than over the Bay of Bengal. The relative humidity of coastal districts in the Indian region rises above 70 percent, and some rain occurs. Above the heated land, the air below 1,500 metres (5,000 feet) becomes unstable, but it is held down by the overriding easterly flow. This does not prevent frequent thunderstorms from occurring in late May.

THE PEAK PERIOD

During June the easterly jet becomes firmly established at 150 to 100 millibars, an atmospheric pressure region typically occurring at elevations between 13,700 and 16,100 metres (45,000 and 53,000 feet). It reaches its greatest speed at its normal position to the south of the anticyclonic ridge, at about 15° N from China through India. In Arabia it decelerates and descends to the middle troposphere (3,000 metres [9,800 feet]). A stratospheric belt of very cold air, analogous to the one normally found above the intertropical convergence near the Equator, occurs above the anticyclonic ridge, across southern Asia at

30°–40° N and above the 500-millibar level (6,000 metres [19,700 feet]). These upper-air features that arise so far away from the Equator are associated with the surface monsoon and are absent when there is no monsoonal flow. The position of the easterly jet controls the location of monsoonal rains, which occur ahead and to the left of the strongest winds and also behind them and to the right. The surface flow, however, is a strong, southwesterly, humid, and unstable wind that brings humidities of more than 80 percent and heavy squally showers that are the "burst" of the monsoon. The overall pattern of the advance follows a frontal alignment, but local episodes may differ considerably. The amount of rain is variable from year to year and place to place.

Most spectacular clouds and rain occur against the Western Ghats in India, where the early monsoonal airstream piles up against the steep slopes, then recedes, and piles up again to a greater height. Each time it pushes thicker clouds upward until wind and clouds roll over the barrier and, after a few brief spells of absorption by the dry inland air, cascade toward the interior. The windward slopes receive 2,000 to 5,000 millimetres (80 to 200 inches) of rain in the monsoon season.

Various factors, especially topography, combine to make up a complex regional pattern. Oceanic air flowing toward India below 6,000 metres (19,700 feet) is deflected in accordance with the Coriolis effect. The converging moist oncoming stream becomes unstable over the hot land and is subject to rapid convection. Towering cumulonimbus clouds rise thousands of metres, producing violent thunderstorms and releasing latent heat in the surrounding air. As a result, the upper tropospheric warm belt migrates northwestward from the ocean to the land. The main body of air above 9,000 metres (29,500 feet) maintains a strong easterly flow.

Later, in June and July, the monsoon is strong and well-established to a height of 6,000 metres (19,700 feet; less in the far north), with occasional thickening to 9,000 metres (29,500 feet). Weather conditions are cloudy, warm, and moist all over India. Rainfall varies between 400 and 500 millimetres (16 and 20 inches), but topography introduces some extraordinary differences. On the southern slopes of the Khasi Hills at only 1,300 metres (4,300 feet), where the moist airstreams are lifted and overturned, the village of Cherrapunji in Meghalaya state receives an average rainfall of 2,730 millimetres (107 inches) in July, with record totals of 897 millimetres (35 inches) in 24 hours in July 1915, more than 9,000 millimetres (354 inches) in July 1861, and 16,305 millimetres (642 inches) in the monsoon season of 1899. Over the Ganges valley the monsoon, deflected by the Himalayan barrier, becomes a southeasterly airflow. By then the upper tropospheric belt of warmth from condensation has moved above northern India, with an oblique bias. The lowest pressures prevail at the surface.

It is mainly in July and August that waves of low pressure appear in the body of monsoonal air. Fully developed depressions appear once or twice per month. They travel from east to west more or less concurrently with high-level easterly waves and bursts of speed from the easterly jet, causing a local strengthening of the low-level monsoonal flow. The rainfall consequently increases and is much more evenly distributed than it was in June. Some of the deeper depressions become tropical cyclones before they reach the land, and these bring torrential rains and disastrous floods.

A totally different development arises when the easterly jet moves farther north than usual. The monsoonal wind rising over the southern slopes of the Himalayas brings heavy rains and local floods. The weather over the

central and southern districts, however, becomes suddenly drier and remains so for as long as the abnormal shift
lasts. The opposite shift is also possible, with midlatitude
upper air flowing along the south face of the Himalayas
and bringing drought to the northern districts. Such dry
spells are known as "breaks" of the monsoon. Those affecting the south of India are similar to those experienced on
the Guinea Coast during extreme northward shifts of the
wind belts, whereas those affecting the north are due to an
interaction of the middle and low latitudes. The southwest monsoon over the lower Indus plain is only 500
metres (about 1,600 feet) thick and does not hold enough
moisture to bring rain. On the other hand, the upper tropospheric easterlies become stronger and constitute a
true easterly jet stream. Western Pakistan, Iran, and
Arabia remain dry (probably because of the divergence in
this jet) and thus become the new source of surface heat.

Monsoon Withdrawal

By August the intensity and duration of sunshine have
decreased, temperatures begin to fall, and the surge of
southwesterly air diminishes spasmodically almost to a
standstill in the northwest. Cherrapunji still receives over
2,000 millimetres (79 inches) of rainfall at this time, however. In September, dry, cool, northerly air begins to circle
the west side of the highlands and spread over northwestern India. The easterly jet weakens, and the upper
tropospheric easterlies move much farther south. Because
the moist southwesterlies at lower levels are much weaker
and variable, they are soon pushed back. The rainfall
becomes extremely variable over most of the region, but
showers are still frequent in the southeastern areas and
over the Bay of Bengal.

By early October, variable winds are very frequent
everywhere. At the end of the month, the entire Indian

region is covered by northerly air and the winter monsoon takes shape. The surface flow is deflected by the Coriolis force and becomes a northeasterly flow. This causes an October–December rainy season for the extreme southeast of the Deccan (including the Madras coast) and eastern Sri Lanka, which cannot be explained by topography alone because it extends well out over the sea. Tropical depressions and cyclones are important contributing factors.

Most of India thus begins a sunny, dry, and dusty season. The driest period comes in November in the Punjab; December in central India, Bengal, and Assam; January in the northern Deccan; and February in the southern Deccan. Conversely, the western slopes of the Karakoram Range and Himalayas are then reached by the midlatitude frontal depressions that come from the Atlantic and the Mediterranean. The winter rains they receive,

Workers transplanting rice near Mangalore, Karnataka, India. Agriculture on the Indian subcontinent frequently depends on summer monsoon rainfall because precipitation during other seasons may be sparse. Baldev/Shostal Associates

moderate as they are, place them clearly outside the monsoonal realm.

Because crops and water supplies depend entirely on monsoonal rains, it became imperative that quantitative long-range weather forecasts be available. Embedded in the weather patterns of other parts of the world are clues to the summer conditions in South Asia. These clues often appear in the months leading up to monsoon onset. For a forecast to be released at the beginning of June, South American pressure and Indian upper-wind data for the month of April are examined. These data, though widely separated from one another, are positively correlated and may be used as predictors of June conditions. Forecasts may be further refined in May by comparing rainfall patterns in both Zimbabwe and Java with the easterly winds above the city of Kolkata (Calcutta) in West Bengal state. In this situation the correlation between rainfall and easterly winds is negative.

The North American Monsoon

The North American monsoon is a seasonal reversal of wind affecting Central America. It is characterized by winds that blow northerly off the Pacific Ocean during warmer months and southerly from the land during cooler months of the year. Although the Gulf Coast of the United States is prone to weather patterns with monsoonal tendencies, consistent winds characteristic of true monsoons are not established there.

In Central America a true monsoonal cycle occurs over a small area facing the Pacific Ocean between 5° and 12° N. Not only is there a complete seasonal reversal of the wind, but the rainfall regime is typically monsoonal. The winter period, from November to January and from March to April according to latitude and other factors, is very dry.

The rainy season begins earlier (in May) in the south and progressively later farther north, coming at the end of June in southern Mexico. It concludes at the end of September in the north and as late as early November in the south. The result is a rainy season that increases in duration with decreasing latitude. It lasts three months in southern Mexico and from six to seven months in Costa Rica. Latitude for latitude, this is a subdued replica of the Indian monsoon.

In North America the relatively low latitude and the orientation of the land-sea boundary on the Gulf of Mexico are quite favourable to monsoonal developments. During the summer, low atmospheric pressure is frequent over the heated land. The northeasterly trade winds are consequently deflected to become easterly, southeasterly, or even southerly winds. In general, Texas and the Gulf Coast of the United States may be completely overrun by a shallow sheet of oceanic air, which may continue for a long distance inland. The rainfall regime does not reveal any marked monsoonal pattern. There are mostly two, three, or even four minor peaks in the sequence of monthly rainfall totals. In the winter there often occur "northers," which are offshore winds caused by the general anticyclonic flow of air from the cold land. Neither the summer onshore wind nor the winter offshore wind is persistent enough to constitute a monsoonal sequence, even though monsoonal tendencies are quite evident.

THE MALAYSIAN-AUSTRALIAN MONSOON

The Malaysian-Australian monsoon is the monsoon system affecting Southeast Asia and Australia. It is characterized by winds that blow from the southeast during cooler months and from the northwest during the warmer months of the year.

GENERAL FEATURES

Southeast Asia and northern Australia are combined in one monsoonal system that differs from others because of the peculiar and somewhat symmetrical distribution of landmasses on both sides of the Equator. In this respect, the northwest monsoon of Australia is unique. The substantial masses of water between Asia and Australia have a moderating effect on tropospheric temperatures, weakening the summer monsoon. The many islands (e.g., Philippines and Indonesia) provide an infinite variety of topographic effects. Typhoons that develop within the monsoonal air bring additional complications.

It would be possible to exclude North China, Korea, and Japan from the monsoonal domain because their seasonal rhythm follows the normal midlatitude pattern—a predominant outflow of cold continental air in winter and frontal depressions and rain alternating with fine, dry anticyclonic weather in the warm season. On the other hand, the seasonal reversal of wind direction in this area is almost as persistent as that in India. The winter winds of northeastern Asia are much stronger because of the relative proximity of the Siberian anticyclone. The tropical ridge of high pressure is the natural boundary between these non-monsoonal areas and the monsoonal lands farther south.

MONSOONAL DEVELOPMENT

The northern limit of the typical monsoon may be set at about 25° N latitude. Farther north the summer monsoon is not strong enough to overcome the effect of the traveling anticyclones normally typical of the subtropics. As a result, monsoonal rains occur in June and also in late August and September, separated by a mild anticyclonic drought in July. In South China and the Philippines the trade winds prevail in the October–April (winter) period, strengthened by the regional, often gusty outflow of air from the stationary Siberian anticyclone. Their disappearance and replacement by opposite (southwesterly) winds in the May–September (summer) period is the essence of the monsoon. In any case, these monsoonal streams are quite shallow, about 1,500 metres (4,900 feet) in winter and 2,000 metres (about 6,600 feet) in summer. They bring rain only when subject to considerable cooling, such as anywhere along the steep windward slopes of the Philippines and Taiwan. On the larger islands there are contrasting effects: the slopes facing west receive most of their rainfall from May to October and experience drought from December to April, whereas the slopes facing east receive orographic rains (those produced when moist air is forced to rise by topography) from September to April and mainly convectional rains from May to October.

Southeast Asia

In Vietnam and Thailand the summer monsoon is more strongly developed because of the wider expanses of over-heated land. The southwesterly stream flows from May to October, reaching a thickness of 4 to 5 kilometres (about 2.5 to 3 miles). It brings plentiful but not extraordinary rainfall. The period from November through February is the cool dry season, and the period from March through April is the hot dry one. In the far south the coolness is but relative. Along the east coast and on the eastward slopes, more rain is brought by the winter monsoon. In the summer, somewhere between Thailand and Cambodia in the interior, there may be a faint line of convergence between the southwesterly Indian-Myanmar monsoon and the southeasterly Malaysian monsoon.

Indonesia

Monsoonal winds are weak over Indonesia because of the expanses of water and the low latitude, but their seasonal reversal is definite. From April to October the Australian southeasterly air flows, whereas north of the Equator the flow becomes southwesterly. The Malaysian-Australian monsoon generally maintains its dryness over the islands closer to Australia, but farther north it carries increasing amounts of moisture. The northeasterly flow from Asia, which becomes northwesterly south of the Equator, is laden with moisture when it reaches Indonesia, bringing cloudy and rainy weather between November and May. The wettest months are December in most of Sumatra and January elsewhere, but rainfall patterns are highly localized. In Java, for instance, at sea level alone there are two major regions: an "equatorial" west with no dry season and a "monsoonal" east with extreme drought in August and September.

Australia

Because of its relatively small size and compact shape, Australia shows relatively simple monsoonal patterns. The north shore is subject to a clear-cut wind reversal between summer (November–April, northwesterly flow) and winter (May–September, southeasterly flow) but with two definite limitations: first, the northwesterly, rain-bearing monsoonal wind is often held offshore and is most likely to override the land to any depth during January and February; second, even in summer there often are prolonged spells of southeasterly trade winds issuing from traveling anticyclones, separating the brief monsoonal incursions. The Australian summer monsoon is thus typical in direction and weather type but quite imperfect in frequency and persistence. Its thickness is usually less than 1,500 metres (4,900 feet) over the sea and 2,000–2,500 metres (6,600–8,200 feet) over the land.

Much less typical are the marginal monsoonal manifestations. On the northwest coast there frequently is a northwesterly airflow in the summer (December–March), as opposed to the winter southeasterlies, but this stream is very shallow and does not bring any rain. That is, its weather is not monsoonal even though its direction is so. On the northeast coast the onshore air is humid and brings rain, but its direction is only partly modified in summer. Most of the summer winds that arrive there occur as a northeasterly flow, although at other times the flow can be mostly southeasterly.

The West African Monsoon

The West African monsoon is a major wind system that affects West African regions between latitudes 9° and 20° N and is characterized by winds that blow southwesterly during warmer months and northeasterly during cooler months of the year. Although areas just outside of this region also experience wind reversals, the influence of the monsoon declines with increasing distance.

General Features

The main characteristics of the West African seasons have been known to the scientific community for more than two centuries. The southwest winter monsoon flows as a shallow humid layer of surface air (less than 2,000 metres [about 6,600 feet]) overlain by the primary northeast trade wind, which blows from the Sahara and the Sahel as a deep stream of dry, often dusty air. As a surface northeasterly, it is generally known as the harmattan, gusty and dry in the extreme, cool at night and scorchingly hot by day. As in a thorough monsoonal development, upper tropospheric anticyclones occur at about 20° N, while the easterly jet stream may occur at about 10° N, much closer to the Equator than they are in the Indian region.

The West African monsoon is the alternation of the southwesterly wind and the harmattan at the surface. Such alternation is normally found between latitudes 9° and 20° N. Northeasterlies occur constantly farther north, but only southwesterlies occur farther south. Except for erratic rains in the high-sun season (June–August), the whole year is more or less dry at 20° N. The drought becomes shorter and less complete farther south. At 12° N it lasts about half the year, and at 8° N it disappears completely. Farther south a different, lighter drought begins to appear in the high-sun months when the monsoonal southwesterly is strongest. This drought results from the arrival of dry surface air issuing from anticyclones formed beyond the Equator in the Southern Hemisphere and is thus similar to the monsoonal drought in Java. Like the "break" of the monsoon in southern India, however, it occurs beyond the Equator.

THE DIFFERENCES FROM OTHER MONSOON SYSTEMS

The moist southwesterly stream, particularly frequent between 5° and 10° N, can reach much farther north, bringing warm humid nights and moderately hot but still humid days. The harmattan brings cooler nights, but the extreme daily heating causes a thermal range of 10–12 °C (18–22 °F). Even in the daytime, the harmattan may give a sensation of coolness to the human skin as it evaporates moisture from the skin's surface. The alternation of the two winds is seasonal on the basis of overall frequency, but in fact it varies considerably with the synoptic pressure patterns. The harmattan comes in spells that mostly last from a few days to more than a week.

The advancing fringe of the southwest monsoon is too shallow (under 1,000 metres [3,300 feet]) for many thunderstorms and other disturbances to occur. They usually occur 200–300 kilometres (about 125–185 miles) behind the fringe, where the moist air is deeper (1,000–2,000 metres [3,300–6,600 feet]) but the ground is still hot enough to make it very unstable. The tops of cumulonimbus clouds may reach 12,000 metres (about 39,000 feet), well above freezing level (4,200–4,500 metres [13,800–14,800 feet]). The disturbances usually occur along a given longitude line that is slightly curved and may in fact form one long line squall. They also reach 12,000 metres (39,000 feet) or more, traveling steadily westward at 37 to 56 kilometres (23 to 35 miles) per hour. This suggests that they originate in the primary trade wind aloft and, as in India, are probably related to the tropical easterly jet stream. The southwest monsoon dominates the weather, and clouds and rain abound. The rain is primarily due to coalescence of droplets, with most of the clouds located below 3,500 metres (11,500 feet). The humidity is very high, and the daily range of temperature remains around 4 °C (7 °F).

If it were not for the change in wind direction when the southeast trades have crossed the Equator, the monsoon system of West Africa could not be distinguished from the weather system, caused by the seasonal shift in the latitude of the intertropical convergence, as experienced over most of Central Africa. There is a rainy season (in this case, the monsoon season), which lasts two to three months at latitude 16° N on the west coast, three to four months at 14° N, six to seven months at 10° N, and eight months at 8° N.

On the south coast, which is at latitude 4° N to 6° N, the southwest monsoon (as the intertropical convergence) may occur at any time, but the results are quite atypical for various reasons. In the low-sun season (December–February), the southwesterly is rare and ineffective, and the weather is cloudy but dry. From April to June, the midday sun is at its highest, and insolation (solar radiation received at Earth's surface) is most intense. Because the southwest wind occurs most frequently, the consequent building up of clouds leads to the main rainy season. During July and August (the short drought), cloudy conditions prevail, but the air issues direct from anticyclones farther south and is dry, in spite of the fact that its direction of flow does not change. Although cloudiness decreases after the second high-sun season in September and October, there is a period of occasional rains just sufficient to constitute a secondary maximum.

Toward the north, conditions are more distinctly monsoonal: by latitude 8° N the two wet seasons have merged into one long "wet" with two subdued peaks, which last approximately seven to eight months (March–October). The "dry," which is controlled by northeast winds, lasts from November to early March. There is one rainfall maximum (in August or September) only a short distance farther north, although the wet season is only a few weeks shorter.

OTHER SIGNIFICANT WINDS

In addition to cyclones, monsoons, and other more well-known manifestations, wind can occur as seasonal phenomena to influence the weather of particular parts of the world. Some winds spiral out of cells of high atmospheric pressure or into cores of low atmospheric pressure. Other winds travel up or down mountain slopes driven by heating and density differences between the air at the surface and the air above.

ANABATIC WINDS

An anabatic wind (also known as an upslope wind) is a local air current that blows up a hill or mountain slope facing the Sun. During the day, the Sun heats such a slope (and the air over it) faster than it does the adjacent atmosphere over a valley or a plain at the same altitude. This warming decreases the density of the air, causing it to rise. More air rises from below to replace it, producing a wind. An anabatic wind may often attain a velocity of more than 6 metres per second (about 13 miles per hour).

BORAS

A bora was originally defined as a very strong, cold wind that blows from the northeast onto the Adriatic region of Italy, Slovenia, and Croatia. The word is from the Greek *boreas,* "northwind." It is most common in winter and occurs when cold air crosses the mountains from the east and descends to the coast. It often reaches speeds of more than 100 kilometres (60 miles) per hour and has been known to knock people down and overturn vehicles.

The name bora is given to similar winds in other parts of Europe, including Bulgaria, the Black Sea, and Novaya Zemlya in the Russian Arctic, and in the western United States along the eastern slopes of the Rocky Mountains.

CYCLOSTROPHIC WINDS

A cyclostrophic wind is a wind circulation that results from a balance between the local atmospheric pressure gradient and the centripetal force.

In small-scale low-pressure systems, such as tornadoes, dust devils, and waterspouts, the radius of curvature of the airflow is relatively small. Cyclostrophic wind flow in these small systems may be either clockwise or counterclockwise, a condition in contrast to larger-scale cyclonic systems, which always rotate in a counterclockwise manner in the Northern Hemisphere and clockwise in the Southern Hemisphere.

Etesian Wind

The etesian wind is a remarkably steady southbound drift of the lower atmosphere over the eastern Mediterranean and adjacent lands in summer. From about mid-May to mid-September, it generally dominates the Adriatic, Ionian, and Aegean seas and the adjacent countries.

The name (from Greek *etos,* "year") is suggestive of the wind's regular recurrence. The wind is of such significance to human activities that the ancient Greeks announced its expected beginning in the marketplaces. An extreme example of its constancy is at Cairo, where July winds blow from the northwest, north, or northeast 98 percent of the time.

The etesian wind, which reaches maximum intensity in the early afternoon and may cease during the night, is part of the general inflow of air toward a low-pressure area usually centred over northwestern India in summer. The wind is actually a dry monsoon wind since it is rainless and not accompanied by high relative humidity. It is not replaced in winter by a steady drift from the opposite direction, and thus the term *monsoon* is not generally used to describe this wind.

Similar wind regimes and climates, called etesian climates and characterized by dry summers and rainy winters, are present in California, Chile, South Africa, and southwestern Australia.

FOEHNS

A foehn is a warm and dry, gusty wind that periodically descends the leeward slopes of nearly all mountains and mountain ranges. The name was first applied to a wind of this kind that occurs in the Alps, where the phenomenon was first studied.

A foehn results from the ascent of moist air up the windward slopes. As this air climbs, it expands and cools until it becomes saturated with water vapour, after which it cools more slowly because its moisture is condensing as rain or snow, releasing latent heat. By the time it reaches the peaks and stops climbing, the air is quite dry. The ridges of the mountains are usually obscured by a bank of clouds known as a foehn wall, which marks the upper limit of precipitation on the windward slopes. As the air makes its leeward descent, it is compressed and warms rapidly all the way downslope because there is little water left to evaporate and absorb heat. Thus, the air is warmer and drier when it reaches the foot of the leeward slope than when it begins its windward ascent.

As previously noted, foehn winds in various parts of the world have local names: chinook in the North American Rockies, *ghibli* in Libya, and *zonda* in the Andes of Argentina.

GRADIENT WINDS

A gradient wind is a wind that accounts for air flow along a curved trajectory. It is an extension of the concept of geostrophic wind—i.e., the wind assumed to move along straight and parallel isobars (lines of equal pressure). The gradient wind represents the actual wind better than does the geostrophic wind, especially when the wind speed and trajectory curvature are large, as they are in hurricanes and jet streams.

The computation of the gradient wind involves a knowledge of curvature in the pressure field on a constant level surface. This information may be derived from the curvature of the isobars. Around a low-pressure centre, the pressure-gradient force directed inward balances the Coriolis force and the centrifugal force, both directed outward. Because the Coriolis force acts to the wind's right in the Northern Hemisphere and to its left in the Southern, the wind blows counterclockwise along the curved isobars in the Northern Hemisphere and clockwise in the Southern Hemisphere. In contrast, around a high-pressure centre, the Coriolis force directed inward balances the centrifugal force and the pressure-gradient force, both directed outward. In this case, the gradient wind blows clockwise along the curved isobars in the Northern Hemisphere and counterclockwise in the Southern Hemisphere.

GREGALES

A gregale, which is also called euroclydon or euraquilo, is a strong and cold wind that blows from the northeast in the western and central Mediterranean region, mainly in winter. Most pronounced on the island of Malta, the gregale sometimes approaches hurricane force and endangers shipping there. In 1555 it is reported to have caused waves that drowned 600 persons in the city of Valletta. A gregale that lasts four or five days is usually the result of a flow of air from central or southern Europe toward Libya. One that lasts only one or two days is caused by the passage of a low-pressure centre over the southern Mediterranean.

HABOOBS

A haboob is a strong wind that occurs primarily along the southern edges of the Sahara in The Sudan. As previously mentioned, it is associated with large sandstorms and duststorms and may be accompanied by thunderstorms. It usually lasts about three hours, is most common during the summer, and may blow from any direction. A haboob may transport huge quantities of sand or dust, which move as a dense wall that can reach a height of 900 metres (about 3,000 feet). Haboobs sometimes also occur in the desert regions of Asia and North America. The term *haboob* is taken from the Arabic word *habb*, meaning "wind."

HARMATTAN

The harmattan, mentioned in sections above, is a hot, dry wind that blows from the northeast or east in the western Sahara and is strongest in late fall and winter (late November to mid-March). It usually carries large amounts of dust, which it transports hundreds of kilometres (miles) out over the Atlantic Ocean. The dust often interferes with aircraft operations and settles on the decks of ships.

The harmattan is a trade wind strengthened by a low-pressure centre over the north coast of the Gulf of Guinea and a high-pressure centre located over northwestern Africa in winter and over the adjacent Atlantic Ocean during other seasons. In the summer it is undercut by the cooler winds of the southwest monsoon, blowing in from the ocean. This forces the harmattan to rise to an altitude of about 900 to 1,800 metres (about 3,000 to 6,000 feet). The interaction between the harmattan and the monsoon sometimes produces West African tornadoes.

KATABATIC WINDS

As noted above, katabatic winds, known alternatively as downslope winds or gravity winds, are currents of air that blow down a slope because of gravity. They occur at night, when the highlands radiate heat and are cooled. The air in contact with these highlands is thus also cooled, and it becomes denser than the air at the same elevation but away from the slope. It therefore begins to flow downhill. This process is most pronounced in calm air because winds mix the air and prevent cold pockets from forming.

When a katabatic wind is warmed by compression during its descent into denser air, it is called a foehn. A large-scale katabatic wind that descends too rapidly to warm up is called a fall wind. In areas where fall winds occur, homes and orchards are situated on hillslopes above the lowlands where the cold air accumulates.

KHAMSIN

The khamsin is a hot, dry, dusty wind in North Africa and the Arabian Peninsula that blows from the south or southeast in late winter and early spring. It often reaches temperatures above 40 °C (104 °F), and it may blow continuously for three or four days at a time and then be followed by an inflow of much cooler air.

The khamsin results when a low-pressure centre moves eastward over the Sahara or the southern Mediterranean Sea. On its forward side, the centre brings warm, dry air northward out of the desert, carrying large amounts of dust and sand. On its rear side, it brings cool air southward from the Mediterranean. The name khamsin is derived from the Arabic word for "50" and refers to the approximately 50-day period in which the wind annually occurs.

LEE WAVES

Lee waves are vertical undulations of airstreams on the lee side of mountains. (The lee side is the side that is downstream from the wind.) The first wave occurs above the mountain that causes it, with a series of waves of equal horizontal wavelength extending downstream. Numerous equally spaced lee waves are often seen where they are not interfered with by other mountains, such as over the sea. They may produce clouds, called wave clouds, when the air becomes saturated with water vapour at the top of the wave.

Lee waves occur most often when a deep airstream with stronger winds in the higher levels and stably stratified air in the lower levels flows across a long ridge having a steep lee slope. The strongest up current then occurs not over the wind-facing slope but at the front of the first lee wave. If the lee slope is very steep and high, the waves may be of sufficient amplitude for a rotor, a vortex with a horizontal axis of rotation perpendicular to the direction of flow, to occur. In a rotor, the wind at the ground blows toward the mountain.

The spacing between the waves is usually around 2 to 8 kilometres (1 to 5 miles). If this spacing coincides approximately with the spacing of the hills, the waves become large. If not, the lee waves of one mountain may be annulled as the air passes over a second. In hilly country with a complicated topography, intense waves may be temporarily set up in one or two places. Strong winds may occur under and upstream of the first lee wave troughs, causing windstorms.

One of the most fully explored and spectacular lee waves is the Sierra wave, which occurs when westerly winds flow over the Sierra Nevada Range in California. It is best developed when the polar-front jet stream blows across the range. In it, gliders have soared to elevations of more than 14,000 metres (45,932 feet).

LEVANTER

The levanter is a strong wind of the western Mediterranean Sea and the southern coasts of France and Spain. It is mild, damp, and rainy and is most common in spring and fall. Its name is derived from Levant, the land at the eastern end of the Mediterranean, and refers to the wind's easterly direction. The levanter reaches its maximum intensities in the Strait of Gibraltar, where it sometimes brings eastward-flying airplanes almost to a standstill. It causes foggy weather on the Spanish coast for up to two days at a time. The levanter results from a merging of the clockwise winds of a high-pressure centre over central Europe with the counterclockwise winds of a low-pressure centre over the southwestern Mediterranean.

MISTRAL

The mistral is a cold and dry, strong wind in southern France that blows down from the north along the lower Rhône River valley toward the Mediterranean Sea. It may blow continuously for several days at a time, attain velocities of about 100 kilometres (60 miles) per hour, and reach to a height of 2 to 3 kilometres (1.3–1.9 miles). It is strongest and most frequent in winter, and it sometimes causes considerable damage to crops. The velocity of the wind is intensified as it blows down from the highlands to the coast and by the "jet effect" that results as it is funneled through the narrow Rhône valley.

POLAR ANTICYCLONE

The wind system associated with a region in which high atmospheric pressure develops over or in the vicinity of the poles is called the polar anticyclone. It is strongest in the cold season of the year. The Siberian anticyclone is an example of a polar anticyclone, as is the high-pressure area that forms over Canada and Alaska during the winter.

Polar anticyclones are created by the cooling of surface layers of air. This cooling causes the air near the surface to become denser and, at the same time, causes an inflow of air at high levels to replace the denser, sinking air. These processes increase the mass of air above the surface, thus creating the anticyclone. The weather within the central regions of these anticyclones is typically clear and quite cold. The strength of polar anticyclones is greatest near the Earth's surface.

Polar anticyclones frequently migrate eastward and equatorward in the winter season, bringing cold waves to warmer latitudes. In the summer they provide cool, dry weather as they move toward the Equator. The boundary separating the cold polar air from the warmer air is called the polar front, and along this frontal surface the extratropical cyclones, or wave cyclones, form.

QUASI-BIENNIAL OSCILLATION

The quasi-biennial oscillation (QBO) is a layer of winds that encircle the Earth in the lower stratosphere, at altitudes from 20 to 40 kilometres (about 12 to 25 miles), between latitudes 15° N and 15° S. They blow at velocities of 25 to 50 metres per second (about 55 to 110 miles per hour). They are alternately easterly and westerly, reversing about every 13 months. The quasi-biennial oscillation was originally known as the Krakatoa winds. This name was derived from the role the winds played in transporting dust thrown into the atmosphere by the explosion (1883) of the volcanic island of Krakatoa in present-day Indonesia.

SHAMAL

The shamal is a hot and dry, dusty wind from the north or northwest in Iraq, Iran, and the Arabian Peninsula. In June and July it blows almost continuously, but usually under 50 kilometres (about 30 miles) per hour. The wind causes great dust storms, especially in July, when Baghdad may experience five or more such storms. The shamal is part of a widespread flow toward a low-pressure centre over Pakistan.

SIBERIAN ANTICYCLONE

The Siberian anticyclone, which is also called the Siberian high, is a semipermanent system of high atmospheric pressure centred in northeastern Siberia during the colder half of the year. The anticyclone forms because of the intense cooling of the surface layers of air over the continent during this season. It is usually quite shallow in vertical extent, rarely persisting to altitudes of 3,000 metres (10,000 feet).

The Siberian anticyclone is one of the principal sources of polar air masses. Mean January temperatures at certain locations within this pressure system are the lowest in the Northern Hemisphere: many stations have averages lower than -46 °C (-51 °F). Outbreaks of polar air westward from this high-pressure area cause occasional severe cold spells in parts of the European continent and eastward across the Arctic Ocean into Alaska and northern Canada. The coldest weather in southern Canada and the 48 contiguous U.S. states is a result of a portion of the Siberian anticyclone traveling south over North America. In the summer, heating over the vast Asian land mass causes the anticyclone to dissipate.

SIMOOM

The simoom, or samum, is an extremely hot and dry local wind in Arabia and the Sahara. Its temperature often reaches 55 °C (about 130 °F), and the humidity of the air sometimes falls below 10 percent. It is caused by intensive ground heating under a cloudless sky. *Simoom* is an Arabic word that means "poison wind." It refers to the wind's tendency to cause heatstroke as it brings more heat to the human body than is removed by the evaporation of perspiration.

SIROCCO

The sirocco is a warm, humid wind occurring over the northern Mediterranean Sea and southern Europe, where it blows from the south or southeast and brings uncomfortably humid air. The sirocco is produced on the east sides of low-pressure centres that travel eastward over the southern Mediterranean. It originates over North Africa as a dry wind and picks up moisture as it crosses the Mediterranean.

TRADE WINDS

The trade winds are persistent currents of air that blow westward and toward the Equator from the subtropical high-pressure belts toward the ITCZ. They are stronger and more consistent over the oceans than over land and often produce partly cloudy sky conditions, characterized by shallow cumulus clouds, or clear skies that make trade-wind islands popular tourist resorts. Their speed averages about 5 to 6 metres per second (11 to 13 miles per hour) but this can increase to speeds of 13 metres per second (30 miles per hour) or more. The trade winds were named by the crews of sailing ships that depended on the winds during westward ocean crossings.

WATERSPOUTS

Waterspouts are small-diameter columns of rapidly swirling air in contact with a water surface. They are almost always produced by a swiftly growing cumulus cloud. They may assume many shapes and often occur in a series, called a waterspout family, produced by the same upward-moving air current. Waterspouts are closely related to other atmospheric phenomena such as tornadoes, whirlwinds, and fire storms.

It is only in recent years that some of the workings of waterspouts have been unraveled, though waterspouts have been known and remarked upon since ancient times. For much of history, they have been subjects of mystery, speculation, and fear. A few intense waterspouts have caused deaths when they moved inland over populated areas, and they certainly constitute a threat to small craft. However, there are few authentic cases of large ships being destroyed by a spout. The superstition that firing a cannonball or other projectile into a spout can "break it up" has no scientific foundation. Contrary to popular opinion, a waterspout does not "suck up" water to great heights, though it may lift the water level 1 metre (3.3 feet) or so at its point of contact with the surface. It is suspected, but remains unproven, that a waterspout may sometimes draw fish and frogs into its vortex and then drop them onto land, thus accounting for the reported falls of such objects.

Modern scientific interest in waterspouts began with the appearance of a particularly large and persistent spout on Aug. 19, 1896, off the coast of Massachusetts, where thousands of vacationers and several scientists observed it. Its height was estimated to be 1,095 metres (3,593 feet, or almost 0.7 mile) and its width, 256 metres (840 feet) at the crest, 43 metres (141 feet) at the centre, and 73 metres (240 feet) at the base. The shroud of spray surrounding the central funnel was about 200 metres (656 feet) wide near the water surface and 120 metres (394 feet) high. The spout's circulation persisted for at least 35 minutes, as the visible funnel disappeared and re-formed three times. Most waterspouts are smaller than this one, with much shorter lives. This exceptional spout is an example of one that apparently was spawned by thunderstorm-squall conditions similar to those that produce tornadoes over land.

There is much confusion in classifying waterspouts. For many years, they were called tornadoes over water, a definition still in wide use. However, as tornado researchers have learned more about atmospheric vortices, it has become clear that several mechanisms can give rise to a strong vortex pendant from a cloud. All of these mechanisms require the following elements: warm, moist, unstable air rising and being replaced at the surface by horizontal convergence of the surrounding air; a rapidly growing cloud aloft; and sufficient rotation in the atmosphere that can be localized and concentrated to produce a vortex. Most waterspouts closely resemble weak tornadoes, some of which are called landspouts because of this similarity. The rotation occurs at low levels in the atmosphere, so the resulting vortex does not extend very far up into the cloud. Indeed, the rotation is not often detectable by radar, another indication that waterspouts are a phenomenon largely confined to the region below cloud base.

Observations from aircraft indicate that most water-spouts have a five-stage life cycle: 1) the dark-spot stage, with a circular, raised patch of water marking the point of contact of the vortex core with the water surface; 2) the spiral-pattern stage, where a spiral is made visible by differences in waves on the water surface; 3) the spray-ring stage, where the dark spot is surrounded by a sheath of water droplets ripped from the water surface by the swirling winds; 4) the mature or spray-vortex stage, where both the spray vortex and the funnel cloud are at their maximum size and intensity; and 5) the decay stage, where the waterspout dissipates.

The main visible feature of a waterspout—the classic inverted cone or funnel—consists mostly of freshwater droplets produced locally by condensation of water vapour. The funnel appears to develop downward from the base of the parent cloud, reaching toward the water surface. The condensation funnel usually appears toward the end of stage 2, as the spiral pattern in the surface water waves wraps tightly around the dark spot marking the centre of the vortex. Frequently the descent of the condensation funnel is followed by the rising of the spray ring from the turbulent water surrounding the dark spot. This sheath often surrounds the lower portion of the funnel. Funnel diameters range from a few metres (feet) to 100 metres (328 feet) or more.

In recent years, efforts have been made to measure the wind speeds in waterspouts. Most researchers have used small airplanes or helicopters to get close to their subjects. By filming or videotaping the swirling condensation funnel or spray sheath, they have been able to track the movement of cloud tag and small clumps of droplets using photogrammetric techniques (measuring the speed of objects recorded on film and assuming that the objects are moving at the same velocity as the wind). Doppler lidar, a

A giant, mature-stage waterspout off the Florida Keys. Waterspouts are closely related to tornadoes, which they greatly resemble. National Oceanic and Atmospheric Administration/Department of Commerce. Archival Photograph by Mr. Steve Nicklas, NOS, NGS

device similar to radar but using light rather than radio waves, has also been used to measure winds in waterspouts. The consensus of these measurements indicates these vortices have winds in the range 15 to 85 metres per second (49 to 279 feet per second), with most spouts having their maximum winds toward the low end of this range. On the Fujita Scale of tornado intensity, most waterspouts would thus rate as F0. That is, almost all waterspouts have intensities similar to those of weak tornadoes.

Measurements of the forward speeds of waterspouts are scarce. Estimates vary from a few kilometres (miles) per hour to as high as 64 to 80 km per hour (40 to 50 miles per hour). Many waterspouts leave a narrow spiral wake of disturbed water as they move along. How this wake, or tail, forms remains unknown.

Waterspouts are most common between late spring and early fall, but they may appear at any time of the year or of the day or night. Lifetimes of typical waterspouts average 5 to 10 minutes, but occasionally a large waterspout may persist for up to one hour.

The worldwide distribution of waterspouts is difficult to determine because most of them occur over oceans, so their detection depends on chance observations from coasts or from ships or airplanes. They are most frequent over tropical and subtropical waters during the warm season. To form, waterspouts require warm surface water in addition to the necessary atmospheric conditions discussed above. Many waterspouts have been observed over the Gulf of Mexico, off the coast of Florida and the Bahamas, and over the Gulf Stream. Indeed, more are reported in the lower Florida Keys than in any other place in the world. Waterspouts are also reported frequently off the west coast of Africa near the Equator and off the coasts of China and Japan. Though they are uncommon at higher latitudes, they have also appeared in places such as the Grand Banks of Newfoundland, on the Great Lakes, and near Seattle, Washington.

WHIRLWINDS

Whirlwinds are small-diameter columnar vortices of rapidly swirling air. A broad spectrum of vortices occurs in the atmosphere, ranging in scale from small eddies that form in the lee of buildings and topographic features to fire storms, waterspouts (discussed separately in the section immediately above), and tornadoes. While the term *whirlwind* can be applied to any atmospheric vortex, it is commonly restricted to atmospheric systems that are smaller than tornadoes but larger than eddies of microscale turbulence. The generic *whirlwind* is usually modified to reflect the visible features associated with the whirl. Thus there are dust whirls or dust devils, sand whirls or sand pillars, and fire, smoke, snow, and even hay whirls.

GENERAL FEATURES

At the centre of the whirlwind, atmospheric pressure is less than it is in the surrounding air, but the decrease is not large. Pressure drops of a few hectopascals (a few tenths of a pound per square inch) are typical in dust devils. (Standard atmospheric pressure at sea level is about 101 kilopascals, or 14.7 pounds per square inch.)

The axis of rotation in a whirlwind is usually vertical, but it may be inclined. In small whirls, the direction of rotation may be either clockwise or counterclockwise. In larger whirls, outside forces may dictate that one direction of rotation dominates.

A mature whirlwind may be divided into three vertical regions. Region 1 is a shallow boundary layer extending up a few tens of centimetres from the ground. It is here that air flows inward, sweeping dust and small detritus into the vortex core. Frictional effects are strong in this layer, limiting the inflow and so preventing the low-pressure core of the vortex from filling from below. Above the shallow boundary layer is Region 2, that of a stable vortex approaching cyclostrophic balance. Cyclostrophic balance is a dynamic equilibrium in which the inward-directed pressure-gradient force is balanced by the outward-directed centrifugal force, allowing air to flow readily around the vortex but not to move easily toward or away from the axis of circulation. Region 3 begins where the top of the vortex becomes destabilized and the turbulent air diffuses with height. Buoyancy forces are strong in Region 3, preventing the vortex core from filling from above. The upper end of a whirlwind almost always terminates in some form of strong convective phenomenon, usually an updraft. Occasionally a very strong dust devil that forms in relatively moist air will terminate in a convective cloud.

Dust Devils

Perhaps the most ubiquitous whirlwind is the dust devil. It is likely that quite a few of these small vortices are present in the lowest several hundred metres (feet) of the atmosphere on many days, but only the rare ones that pick up detritus from the surface are seen. Certainly every summer, hundreds of thousands of dust devils form and travel across the arid and semiarid regions of the world. Observers report dust whirls almost daily during the hot season over the Sahara as well as the arid regions of Australia and the southwestern United States. They also are common over sections of India and the Middle East.

Dust devils occur most frequently under hot, clear-sky conditions with light winds. Such environments give rise to a strong heat flux from the hot surface of the Earth to the lowest layers of the atmosphere. This energy is absorbed by the atmosphere to produce a highly unstable layer near the ground. Release of the energy stored in this unstable layer leads to the formation of thermal plumes (large parcels of hot air rising from the surface). A dust devil draws on this stored energy to develop and then maintain itself. A light wind is required to start rotation in the rising plume. When dissipative forces, such as surface friction and eddy interaction with the environment, exceed the available energy, the whirlwind is destroyed.

The stability of the surface layer of the atmosphere does not depend on its actual temperature, but on the rate of change of temperature with height in the layer. Any process that produces an unstable surface layer can give rise to thermal plumes and to whirlwinds. This accounts for the sighting of dust devils and related whirls under temperate conditions and even in cool conditions such as those of the subarctic. Dust devils have even been observed on Mars, where temperatures are much colder than on Earth.

This dependence on instability of the surface air layer is the reason dust devils are usually most active in the early afternoon, from 12:30 to 2 PM. During this period the heated ground surface attains its peak temperature and, therefore, the surface layer its greatest instability.

Dust devils often appear in groups or series. Eleven of them were simultaneously sighted in Ethiopia. In the Mojave Desert in eastern California, a series of smaller whirls were seen following in the wake of a larger primary vortex. In India, such secondary vortices are sometimes called dancing devils. Such clusters of vortices are probably tied to a large thermal plume passing by.

The shape of the central core of the dust devil, as revealed by lofted dust, is normally that of a cylindrical column or an inverted cone. The diameter of the visible core can be anywhere from several centimetres to a few hundred metres. The diameter of the actual column of swirling air may be five to ten times greater than the diameter of the core. Dust devils have visible heights ranging from a few metres to at least 1,500 metres (4,900 feet, or 0.9 mile). This is probably not the upper limit on height. Sailplane pilots have used their upward-spiraling currents to soar to above 4,500 metres (15,000 feet, or 2.8 miles).

Though dust devils can last from several seconds to about seven hours, the duration of most is probably less than five minutes. Few persist for more than one hour. Larger, more vigorous whirls have a longer lifetime than smaller vortices. One large dust devil, with a height of about 750 metres (2,500 feet), persisted for seven hours as it traveled 64 kilometres (40 miles) on salt flats in western Utah. In northwestern Mexico a large whirl reportedly formed at the end of an embankment and remained there for four hours. The life of a dust devil may be longer than visual observations indicate, because the vortex dynamics are independent of the materials borne aloft that make its presence obvious to the eye.

For many years, the wind speeds in dust devils were unknown. Observers' reports indicated that vertical wind speeds were sufficiently strong to lift small objects, including jackrabbits. In recent years, researchers using probes, cameras, and videotape equipment have estimated the speeds in the vortex core. In moderately strong vortices, wind speeds of 40 kilometres per hour (25 miles per hour) flowing around the centre of rotation have been measured and are probably common. Velocities of more than 80 kilometres per hour (50 miles per hour) probably occur in some of the larger, more vigorous dust devils. Sailplane pilots have measured vertical speeds of 16 kilometres per hour (10 miles per hour) in moderate whirls and 32 to 48 kilometres per hour (20 to 30 miles per hour) in stronger vortices.

Chapter 3

THUNDERSTORMS

Thunderstorms are violent, short-lived weather disturbances that are almost always associated with lightning, thunder, dense clouds, heavy rain or hail, and strong, gusty winds. They arise when layers of warm, moist air rise in a large, swift updraft to cooler regions of the atmosphere. There the moisture contained in the updraft condenses to form towering cumulonimbus clouds and, eventually, precipitation. Columns of cooled air then sink earthward, striking the ground with strong downdrafts and horizontal winds. At the same time, electrical charges accumulate on cloud particles (water droplets and ice). Lightning discharges occur when the accumulated electric charge becomes sufficiently large. Lightning heats the air it passes through so intensely and quickly that shock waves (heard as thunder) are produced. On occasion, severe thunderstorms are accompanied by swirling vortices of air that become concentrated and powerful enough to form tornadoes.

Thunderstorms are known to occur in almost every region of the world, though they are rare in polar regions and infrequent at latitudes higher than 50° N and 50° S. The temperate and tropical regions of the world, therefore, are the most prone to thunderstorms. In the United States the areas of maximum thunderstorm activity are the Florida peninsula (more than 90 thunderstorm days per year), the Gulf Coast (70–80 days per year), and the mountains of New Mexico (50–60 days per year). Central Europe and Asia average 20 to 60 thunderstorm days per year. It has been estimated that at any one moment there are approximately 1,800 thunderstorms in progress throughout the world.

This chapter covers two major aspects of thunderstorms: their meteorology (i.e., their formation, structure, and distribution) and their electrification (i.e., the generation of lightning and thunder).

THUNDERSTORM FORMATION AND STRUCTURE

Most brief but violent disturbances in Earth's wind systems involve large areas of ascending and descending air. Thunderstorms are no exception to this pattern. In technical terms, a thunderstorm is said to develop when the atmosphere becomes "unstable to vertical motion." Such an instability can arise whenever relatively warm, light air is overlain by cooler, heavier air. Under such conditions the cooler air tends to sink, displacing the warmer air upward. If a sufficiently large volume of air rises, an updraft (a strong current of rising air) will be produced. If the updraft is moist, the water will condense and form clouds. Condensation in turn will release latent heat energy, further fueling upward air motion and increasing the instability.

Once upward air motions are initiated in an unstable atmosphere, rising parcels of warm air accelerate as they rise through their cooler surroundings because they have a lower density and are more buoyant. This motion can set up a pattern of convection wherein heat and moisture are transported upward and cooler and drier air is transported downward. Areas of the atmosphere where vertical motion is relatively strong are called cells, and when they carry air to the upper troposphere (the lowest layer of the atmosphere), they are called deep cells. Thunderstorms develop when deep cells of moist convection become organized and merge, and then produce precipitation and ultimately lightning and thunder.

Upward motions can be initiated in a variety of ways in the atmosphere. A common mechanism is by the heating of a land surface and the adjacent layers of air by sunlight. If surface heating is sufficient, the temperatures of the lowest layers of air will rise faster than those of layers aloft, and the air will become unstable. The ability of the ground to heat up quickly is why most thunderstorms form over land rather than oceans. Instability can also occur when

A cumulonimbus cloud displaying the anvil shape up top and darkened base that precede a thunderstorm with heavy downpours. National Oceanic and Atmospheric Administration/Department of Commerce. Photograph by Indianapolis Times

layers of cool air are warmed from below after they move over a warm ocean surface or over layers of warm air. Mountains, too, can trigger upward atmospheric motion by acting as topographic barriers that force winds to rise. Mountains also act as high-level sources of heat and instability when their surfaces are heated by the Sun.

The huge clouds associated with thunderstorms typically start as isolated cumulus clouds (clouds formed by convection, as described above) that develop vertically into domes and towers. If there is enough instability and moisture and the background winds are favourable, the heat released by condensation will further enhance the buoyancy of the rising air mass. The cumulus clouds will grow and merge with other cells to form a cumulus congestus cloud extending even higher into the atmosphere (6,000 metres [20,000 feet] or more above the surface). Ultimately, a cumulonimbus cloud will form, with its characteristic anvil-shaped top, billowing sides, and dark base. Cumulonimbus clouds typically produce large amounts of precipitation.

TYPES OF THUNDERSTORMS

At one time, thunderstorms were classified according to where they occurred—for example, as local, frontal, or orographic (mountain-initiated) thunderstorms. Today it is more common to classify storms according to the characteristics of the storms themselves, and such characteristics depend largely on the meteorological environment in which the storms develop. The United States National Weather Service has defined a severe thunderstorm as any storm that produces a tornado, winds greater than 26 metres per second (94 kilometres [58 miles] per hour), or hail with a diameter greater than 1.9 centimetres (0.75 inch).

ISOLATED THUNDERSTORMS

Isolated thunderstorms tend to occur where there are light winds that do not change dramatically with height and where there is abundant moisture at low and middle levels of the atmosphere—that is, from near the surface of the ground up to around 10,000 metres (33,000 feet) in altitude. These storms are sometimes called air-mass or local thunderstorms. They are mostly vertical in structure, are relatively short-lived, and usually do not produce violent weather at the ground. Aircraft and radar measurements show that such storms are composed of one or more convective cells, each of which goes through a well-defined life cycle. Early in the development of a cell, the air motions are mostly upward, not as a steady, uniform stream but as one that is composed of a series of rising eddies. Cloud and precipitation particles form and grow as the cell grows. When the accumulated load of water and ice becomes excessive, a downdraft starts. The downward motion is enhanced when the cloud particles evaporate and cool the air—almost the reverse of the processes in an updraft. At maturity, the cell contains both updrafts and downdrafts in close proximity. In its later stages, the downdraft spreads throughout the cell and diminishes in intensity as precipitation falls from the cloud. Isolated thunderstorms contain one or more convective cells in different stages of evolution. Frequently, the downdrafts and associated outflows from a storm trigger new convective cells nearby, resulting in the formation of a multiple-cell thunderstorm.

Solar heating is an important factor in triggering local, isolated thunderstorms. Most such storms occur in the late afternoon and early evening, when surface temperatures are highest.

MULTIPLE-CELL THUNDERSTORMS
AND MESOSCALE CONVECTIVE SYSTEMS

Violent weather at the ground is usually produced by organized multiple-cell storms, squall lines, or a supercell. All of these tend to be associated with a mesoscale disturbance (a weather system of intermediate size, that is, 10 to 1,000 kilometres [6 to 600 miles] in horizontal extent). Multiple-cell storms have several updrafts and downdrafts in close proximity to one another. They occur in clusters of cells in various stages of development moving together as a group. Within the cluster one cell dominates for a time before weakening, and then another cell repeats the cycle. In squall lines, thunderstorms form in an organized line and create a single, continuous gust front (the leading edge of a storm's outflow from its downdraft). Supercell storms have one intense updraft and downdraft.

Sometimes the development of a mesoscale weather disturbance causes thunderstorms to develop over a region hundreds of kilometres (miles) in diameter. Examples of such disturbances include frontal wave cyclones (low-pressure systems that develop from a wave on a front separating warm and cool air masses) and low-pressure troughs at upper levels of the atmosphere. The resulting pattern of storms is called a mesoscale convective system (MCS). Severe multiple-cell thunderstorms and supercell storms are frequently associated with MCSs. Precipitation produced by these systems typically includes rainfall from convective clouds and from stratiform clouds (cloud layers with a large horizontal extent). Stratiform precipitation is primarily due to the remnants of older cells with a relatively low vertical velocity—that is, with limited convection occurring.

Thunderstorms can be triggered by a cold front that moves into moist, unstable air. Sometimes squall lines develop in the warm air mass tens to hundreds of kilometres ahead of a cold front. The tendency of prefrontal storms to be more or less aligned parallel to the front indicates that they are initiated by atmospheric disturbances caused by the front.

In the central United States, severe thunderstorms commonly occur in the springtime, when cool westerly winds at middle levels (3,000 to 10,000 metres [10,000 to 33,000 feet] in altitude) move over warm and moist surface air flowing northward from the Gulf of Mexico. The resulting broad region of instability produces MCSs that persist for many hours or even days.

In the tropics, the northeast trade winds meet the southeast trades near the Equator, and the resulting intertropical convergence zone (ITCZ) is characterized by air that is both moist and unstable. Thunderstorms and MCSs appear in great abundance in the ITCZ. They play an important role in the transport of heat to upper levels of the atmosphere and to higher latitudes.

SUPERCELL STORMS

When environmental winds are favourable, the updraft and downdraft of a storm become organized and twist around and reinforce each other. The result is a long-lived supercell storm. These storms are the most intense type of thunderstorm. In the central United States, supercells typically have a broad, intense updraft that enters from the southeast and brings moist surface air into the storm. The updraft rises, rotates counterclockwise, and exits to the east, forming an anvil. Updraft speeds in supercell storms can exceed 40 metres (130 feet) per second and are capable of suspending hailstones as large as grapefruit. Supercells can last two to six hours. They are the most likely storm to produce spectacular wind and hail damage as well as powerful tornadoes.

THE PHYSICAL CHARACTERISTICS OF THUNDERSTORMS

Aircraft and radar measurements show that a single thunderstorm cell extends to an altitude of 8,000 to 10,000 metres (26,000 to 33,000 feet) and lasts about 30 minutes. An isolated storm usually contains several cells in different stages of evolution and lasts about an hour. A large storm can be many tens of kilometres in diameter with a top that extends to altitudes above 18 kilometres (10 miles), and its duration can be many hours.

UPDRAFTS AND DOWNDRAFTS

The updrafts and downdrafts in isolated thunderstorms are typically between about 0.5 and 2.5 kilometres (0.3 and 1.6 miles) in diameter at altitudes of 3 to 8 kilometres (1.9 to 5 miles). The updraft diameter may occasionally exceed 4 kilometres (2.5 miles). Closer to the ground, drafts tend to have a larger diameter and lower speeds than do drafts higher in the cloud. Updraft speeds typically peak in the range of 5 to 10 metres (16 to 33 feet) per second, and speeds exceeding 20 metres (66 feet) per second are common in the upper parts of large storms. Airplanes flying through large storms at altitudes of about 10,000 metres (33,000 feet) have measured updrafts exceeding 30 metres (98 feet) per second. The strongest updrafts occur in organized storms that are many tens of kilometres in diameter, and lines or zones of such storms can extend for hundreds of kilometres.

DOWNBURSTS

Sometimes thunderstorms will produce intense down-drafts that create damaging winds on the ground. These downdrafts are referred to as macrobursts or microbursts, depending on their size. A macroburst is more than 4 kilo-metres (2.5 miles) in diameter and can produce winds as high as 60 metres per second, or 215 kilometres per hour (200 feet per second, or 135 miles per hour). A microburst is smaller in dimension but produces winds as high as 75 metres per second, or 270 kilometres per hour (250 feet

Microburst

A microburst is a pattern of intense winds that descends from rain clouds, hits the ground, and fans out horizontally. Microbursts are short-lived, usually lasting from about 5 to 15 minutes, and they are relatively compact, usually affecting an area of 1 to 3 kilometres (about 0.5 to 2 miles) in diameter. They are often but not always associated with thunderstorms or strong rains. By causing a sudden change in wind direction or speed—a condition known as wind shear—microbursts create a particular hazard for airplanes at takeoff and landing because the pilot is confronted with a rapid and unexpected shift from headwind to tailwind.

In arid regions, the rain commonly associated with micro-bursts often evaporates before the downdraft reaches the ground. The resulting dry microbursts produce no visible clue to their presence. Wet microbursts, typical of more humid areas, are generally accompanied by a visible rain shaft. Bursts can be detected by modern weather radar and by wind sensors on the ground. The mechanics of microburst phenomena are not yet completely understood. Their existence was first observed in 1974 by meteorologist T. Theodore Fujita, and since then they have been identified as the cause of several airline crashes.

per second, or 170 miles per hour) on the ground. When the parent storm forms in a wet, humid environment, the microburst will be accompanied by intense rainfall at the ground. If the storm forms in a dry environment, however, the precipitation may evaporate before it reaches the ground (such precipitation is referred to as virga), and the microburst will be dry.

VERTICAL EXTENT

In general, an active cloud will rise until it loses its buoyancy. A loss of buoyancy is caused by precipitation loading when the water content of the cloud becomes heavy enough, or by the entrainment of cool, dry air, or by a combination of these processes. Growth can also be stopped by a capping inversion, that is, a region of the atmosphere where the air temperature decreases slowly, is constant, or increases with height.

Thunderstorms typically reach altitudes above 10,000 metres (33,000 feet) and sometimes more than 20,000 metres (66,000 feet). When the instability is high, the atmosphere moist, and winds favourable, thunderstorms can extend to the tropopause, that is, the boundary between the troposphere and the stratosphere. The tropopause is characterized by air temperatures that are nearly constant or increasing with height, and it is a region of great stability. Occasionally the momentum of an updraft carries it into the stratosphere, but after a short distance the air in the top of the updraft becomes cooler and heavier than the surrounding air, and the overshoot ceases. The height of the tropopause varies with both latitude and season. It ranges from about 10,000 to 15,000 metres (33,000 to 50,000 feet) and is higher near the Equator.

Turbulence

An airplane flying through a thunderstorm is commonly buffeted upward and downward and from side to side by turbulent drafts in a storm. Atmospheric turbulence causes discomfort for the crew and passengers and also subjects the aircraft to undesirable stresses.

Turbulence can be quantified in various ways, but frequently a g unit, equal to the acceleration of gravity (9.8 metres per second squared, or 32.2 feet per second squared), is used. A gust of one g will cause severe aircraft turbulence. In the upper part of violent thunderstorms, vertical accelerations of about three g have been reported.

When a cumulonimbus cloud reaches a capping inversion or the tropopause, it spreads outward and forms the anvil cloud so characteristic of most thunderstorms. The winds at anvil altitudes typically carry cloud material downwind, and sometimes there are weak cells of convection embedded in the anvil.

THE MOVEMENT OF THUNDERSTORMS

The motion of a thunderstorm across the land is determined primarily by the interactions of its updrafts and downdrafts with steering winds in the middle layers of the atmosphere in which the storm develops. The speed of isolated storms is typically about 20 kilometres (12 miles) per hour, but some storms move much faster. In extreme circumstances, a supercell storm may move 65 to 80 kilometres (about 40 to 50 miles) per hour. Most storms continually evolve and have new cells developing while old ones dissipate. When winds are light, an individual cell may move very little, less than 2 kilometres (1.2 miles), during its lifetime. However, in a larger storm, new cells triggered by the outflow from downdrafts can give the appearance of rapid motion. In large, multicell storms, the new cells tend to form to the right of the steering winds in the Northern Hemisphere and to the left in the Southern Hemisphere.

Energy

The energy that drives thunderstorms comes primarily from the latent heat that is released when water vapour condenses to form cloud drops. For every gram of water that is condensed, about 600 calories of heat are released to the atmosphere. When water drops freeze in the upper parts of the cloud, another 80 calories per gram are released. The release of latent heat energy in an updraft is converted, at least in part, to the kinetic energy of the air motions. A rough estimate of the total energy in a thunderstorm can be made from the total quantity of water that is precipitated by the cloud. In a typical case, this energy is about 10^7 kilowatt-hours, roughly equivalent of a 20-kiloton nuclear explosion (though it is released over a broader area and in a longer span of time). A large, multicell storm can easily be 10 to 100 times more energetic.

The Weather Under Thunderstorms

The weather conditions underneath thunderstorms are often driven by the vertical motion of air. The cooled air above descends because it is more dense than the air below. Sometimes this downward movement is rapid enough to produce strong gusts that travel horizontally over the ground. Also, the area underneath a cumulonimbus cloud is the site of significant, sometimes torrential, rainfall.

DOWNDRAFTS AND GUST FRONTS

Thunderstorm downdrafts originate at altitudes where the air temperature is cooler than at ground level, and they are kept cool even as they sink to warmer levels by the evaporation of water and melting of ice particles. Not only is the sinking air more dense than its surroundings, but it carries a horizontal momentum that is different from the surrounding air. If the descending air originated at a height of 10,000 metres (33,000 feet), for example, it might reach the ground with a horizontal velocity much higher than the wind at the ground. When such air hits the ground, it usually moves outward ahead of the storm at a higher speed than the storm itself. This is why an observer on the ground watching a thunderstorm approach can often feel a gust of cool air before the storm passes overhead. The outspreading downdraft air forms a pool some 500 to 2,000 metres (about 1,600 to 6,500 feet) deep, and often there is a distinct boundary between the cool air and the warm, humid air in which the storm developed. The passage of such a gust front is easily recognized as the wind speed increases and the air temperature suddenly drops. Over a five-minute period, a cooling of more than 5 °C (9 °F) is not unusual, and cooling twice as great is not unknown.

In extreme circumstances, the gust front produced by a downburst may reach 50 metres (about 160 feet) per second or more and do extensive damage to property and vegetation. Severe winds occur most often when organized lines of thunderstorms develop in an environment where the middle-level winds are very strong. Under such conditions, people might think the winds were caused by a tornado. If a funnel cloud is not observed, the character of the wind damage can indicate the source. Tornadoes blow debris in a tight circular pattern, whereas the air from a thunderstorm outflow pushes it mostly in one direction.

RAINFALL

By the time the cool air arrives, rain usually is reaching the surface. Sometimes all the raindrops evaporate while falling, and the result is a dry thunderstorm. At the other extreme, severe multiple-cell and supercell storms can produce torrential rain and hail and cause flash floods.

In small thunderstorms, peak five-minute rainfall rates can exceed 120 millimetres (4.7 inches) per hour, but most rainfalls are about one-tenth this amount. The average thunderstorm produces about 2,000 metric tons (220,000 short tons) of rain, but large storms can produce 10 times more rainfall. Large, organized storms that are associated with mesoscale convective systems can generate 10^{10} to 10^{12} kg of rainfall.

THUNDERSTORM ELECTRIFICATION

Within a single thunderstorm, there are updrafts and downdrafts and a variety of cloud particles and precipitation. Measurements show that thunderclouds in different geographic locations tend to produce an excess negative charge at altitudes where the ambient air temperature is between about -5 and -15 °C (23 to 5 °F). Positive charge accumulates at both higher and lower altitudes. The result is a division of charge across space that creates a high electric field and the possibility of significant electrical activity.

Many mechanisms have been proposed to explain the overall electrical structure of a thunderstorm, and cloud electrification is an active area of research. A leading hypothesis is that if the larger and heavier cloud particles charge preferentially with a negative polarity, and the smaller and lighter particles acquire a positive polarity, then the separation between positive and negative regions occurs simply because the larger particles fall faster than the lighter cloud constituents. Such a mechanism is generally consistent with laboratory studies that show electrical charging when soft hail, or graupel particles (porous amalgamations of frozen water droplets), collide with ice crystals in the presence of supercooled water droplets. The amount and polarity of the graupel charges depend on the ambient air temperature and on the liquid water content of the cloud, as well as on the ice crystal size, the velocity of the collision, and other factors. Other mechanisms of electrification are also possible.

LIGHTNING OCCURRENCE

When the accumulated electric charges in a thunderstorm become sufficiently large, lightning discharges take place between opposite charge regions, between charged regions and the ground, or from a charged region to the neutral atmosphere. In a typical thunderstorm, roughly two-thirds of all discharges occur within the cloud, from cloud to cloud, or from cloud to air. The rest are between the cloud and ground.

In recent years it has become clear that lightning can be artificially initiated, or triggered, in clouds that would not normally produce natural lightning discharges. Lightning can be triggered by a mountain or a tall

Lightning flash striking a tree at a distance of 60 metres (200 feet) from the camera. Richard E. Orville

structure when a thunderstorm is overhead and there is a high electric field in the vicinity or when an aircraft or large rocket flies into a high-field environment.

Lightning Distribution in the United States

Every year, most of the United States experiences at least two cloud-to-ground strikes per square kilometre (about five per square mile). Most of the interior of the country east of the Rocky Mountains has four or more strikes per square kilometre (about 10 discharges per square mile). Summer thunderstorms are frequent in northern Mexico and the states of Arizona, New Mexico, and Colorado when warm, humid air is forced to rise by mountainous terrain.

Maximum flash densities are found along the Gulf Coast and Florida peninsula, where over a year's time, values exceeding 10 strikes per square kilometre (25 strikes per square mile) have been measured. More than 20 million cloud-to-ground flashes strike the United States annually, and lightning is clearly among the country's most severe weather hazards.

Global Lightning Distribution

Data from Earth-orbiting satellites show that, on average, about 80 percent of lightning flashes occur over land and 20 percent over the oceans. The frequency of lightning over land tends to peak in the mid-afternoon between 3 PM and 6 PM local time. Seasonal trends in the distribution of lightning are the result of temperature changes at the Earth's surface.

Tropical air masses commonly produce thunderstorms and lightning. Thunderstorm development requires moist, unstable air masses typical of those in tropical areas. In this region the Sun's rays are nearly vertical, allowing more energy to reach and warm the lowest layers of the atmosphere. Abundant moisture is added when the warm air moves over the ocean and becomes humidified by evaporation from the underlying water surface. Thunderstorm development is then initiated by upward movement of air, due to, for example, changes in air pressure or the topography of the land. The average number of days with audible thunder exceeds 100 per year over land areas within 10 degrees latitude north and south of the Equator. In some regions of equatorial Africa and South America there are more than 180 thunder days in an average year.

At higher latitudes, thunderstorm frequency depends on the character of the topography and how often moist, tropical air invades the region, which happens most often in the spring and summer. Maximum thunderstorm activity in the Northern and Southern Hemispheres is offset by approximately six months, with most Northern Hemisphere thunderstorms occurring between May and September and in the Southern Hemisphere between November and March.

Thunderstorms are a common feature of the summer monsoons in many parts of the world, especially southern Asia. As solar radiation warms the Indian subcontinent, an ocean-to-land air current is established and moist, unstable air from the Indian Ocean is carried inland. When this air is forced to rise by the steep slopes of the Himalayas, intense thunderstorms and rain showers are produced in great abundance.

In regions poleward of about 60 degrees latitude thunderstorms are rare to nonexistent. In these regions the air near the surface is cold and the atmosphere is generally stable. There are also few thunderstorms in regions that are dominated by semipermanent high-pressure centres, such as southern California. In these regions air from higher altitudes is descending and warming, which lowers the relative humidity and causes stable stratification of the lower atmosphere. As a result, thunderstorm development is inhibited.

CLOUD-TO-GROUND LIGHTNING

The production of lightning between a cloud and the ground involves the creation of air channels within which initial and return strokes of lightning travel. Thunder, the crashing sound that accompanies lightning, is the result of the shock wave created by the return stroke.

INITIAL STROKE

A typical flash of cloud-to-ground lightning is initiated by electrical breakdown between the small positive charge region near the base of the cloud and the negative charge region in the middle of the cloud. The preliminary breakdown creates channels of air that have undergone partial ionization—the conversion of neutral atoms and molecules to electrically charged ones.

On timescales measured in fractions of a second, high-speed cameras can record luminous events in the flash. Initially, a faint luminous process descends in a downward-branching pattern in regular distinct steps, typically 30 metres (100 feet) in length, though they can range from 10 to 100 metres (33 to 330 feet). The time interval between steps ranges from 10 to 50 microseconds (millionths of a second). Carrying currents on the order of hundreds to thousands of amperes, the stepped leader propagates toward the ground at an average velocity of 1.5×10^5 metres (492,126 feet) per second, or about one two-thousandth the speed of light. It is called a stepped leader because of its downward-moving "stepped" pulses of luminosity. Diameter estimates for the stepped leader range from a few centimetres to a few metres. The current-carrying core has a diameter on the order of 1 or 2 centimetres (0.4 or 0.8 inch), and photographic measurements indicate that a corona sheath of electric charge with a diameter of 1 to 10 metres (3 to 33 feet) surrounds the core.

RETURN STROKE

As the stepped leader nears the ground, approximately five coulombs of charge have been deposited along the channel, inducing an opposite charge on the ground and increasing the electric field between the leader and the point to be struck. An upward discharge starts at the ground, church steeple, house, or other object, and rises to meet the stepped leader about 15 to 50 metres (50 to 160 feet) above the surface. At this moment of junction the cloud is short-circuited to the ground and a highly luminous return stroke of high current occurs. It is this return stroke, rather than the stepped leader, that is perceived as lightning because it is so much brighter and follows so quickly after the stepped leader. Portions of the stepped leader that have not reached the ground become the branches of the return stroke, and charge on the branches flows into the main channel.

The five coulombs of charge typically deposited along the stepped leader flow to ground in a few hundred microseconds and produce peak currents that are usually on the order of 30,000 amperes but may range from a few thousand to over 200,000 amperes. Peak temperatures in the channel are on the order of 30,000 °C (50,000 °F), about five times hotter than the surface of the Sun. Because the junction process occurs near the ground, the time to peak current measured at the ground is typically only a few microseconds. As the leader charge avalanches toward the ground, the return stroke luminosity propagates toward the cloud base at an average speed of 5×10^7 to 2×10^8 metres (164,041,995 to 656,167,979 feet) per second, or approximately one-third the speed of light, and the high-current-carrying core expands to a diameter of a few centimetres. Laboratory experiments suggest that when pressure equilibrium is attained between the return stroke and the surrounding air, the channel approximates a high-current arc characterized by a current density of 1,000 amperes per square centimetre (.15 square inch).

Subsequent Return Strokes

In the rapid passage from ground to cloud, the luminous return stroke is observed to pause at points where large branches join the main channel, and the channel is observed to brighten as charge from the branch flows into the channel. The stroke then continues its upward propagation, reaching the level of the atmosphere where the temperature is 0 °C (32 °F; typically at an altitude of 5 kilometres [3 miles] above sea level) in approximately 100 microseconds. The downward-propagating stepped leader traverses the same distance in about 30 milliseconds (thousandths of a second). There is then a pause for tens of milliseconds, and the channel cools to a few thousand degrees Celsius. If a second stroke occurs, it begins with the appearance of a dart of light, perhaps 30 to 50 metres (100 to 160 feet) in length, propagating down the channel of the previous return stroke. The dart leader moves downward at a speed of 2×10^6 metres per second (6,561,680 feet per second; about one one-hundredth the speed of light) and carries a current of the order of 1,000 amperes toward the ground. Once again, when the leader effectively short-circuits a charge centre in the cloud to the ground, another return stroke occurs. After the first stroke, the dart leader may follow the lightning channel only partway before taking a new path to the ground. This gives rise to the common forked appearance of lightning as it strikes the ground.

This sequence of dart leader-return stroke typically occurs three to four times, although a flash to the ground that had 26 strokes and lasted two seconds has been reported. When a flash does have more than one stroke, the subsequent return strokes draw charge from different regions of the parent thunderstorm. Multiple strokes of lightning appear to flicker because the human eye is just capable of resolving the time interval between them.

THE DISSIPATION OF ENERGY

During the return-stroke stage, approximately 10^5 joules of energy per metre are dissipated within the lightning channel. This energy is divided among the dissociation, ionization, excitation, and kinetic energy of the particles, the energy of expansion of the channel, and radiation. Spectroscopic measurements reveal that the air molecules, principally those of nitrogen, oxygen, and water, are split into their respective atoms and that on the average one electron is removed from each atom. The conversion from neutral air molecules to a completely ionized plasma occurs in a few microseconds.

THUNDER

When the stroke plasma is created, its temperature is at least 30,000 °C (50,000 °F), and the pressure is greater than 1,000 kilopascals (10 atmospheres). The channel pressure greatly exceeds the ambient (surrounding) pressure, and the return-stroke channel expands at a supersonic rate. The resultant shock wave decays rapidly with distance and is eventually heard as thunder once it slows to the speed of sound. Because it is estimated that only 1 percent of the input energy is stored in the particles and less than 1 percent is emitted as radiation in the visible and infrared region (4,000 to 11,000 angstroms [Å], where Å = 10⁻¹⁰ metre [3.3 x 10⁻¹⁰ feet]), it is probable that most of the energy dissipated goes into the energy of channel expansion, a process requiring no more than 10 to 20 microseconds.

Since light travels at about 300,000 kilometres (186,000 miles) per second and the speed of sound is only about 0.33 kilometres (0.2 mile) per second, the light from a discharge will always be seen before the sound arrives at an observer. The time delay between the bright flash of light and the arrival of the associated thunder can often be used to estimate the distance to a discharge. Every three seconds correspond to one kilometre, and every five seconds correspond to one mile.

The total thunder waveform comes from the entire lightning channel and includes the effects of channel branching and tortuosity, sound propagation in the atmosphere, and acoustic reflections from the local topography. The result is a series of sounds that are variously described as peaks, claps, rolls, and rumbles. At distances of a few hundred metres (feet), thunder begins with a sudden clap followed by a long rumble. At larger distances, it begins with a rumble.

TRIGGERED LIGHTNING

A small percentage of discharges between the cloud and ground are actually initiated at the ground and propagate upward to a charged region in the cloud. These discharges often are initiated (or triggered) by tall structures or by towers on hilltops. The upward branching of such discharges makes them visually distinguishable from their "right-side-up" counterparts, giving the impression of a cloud-to-ground lightning flash that is upside down.

Lightning discharge triggered by the presence of a tall tower atop Mount San Salvatore, near Lugano, Switzerland. Courtesy of Richard E. Orville

CLOUD-TO-CLOUD AND INTRACLOUD LIGHTNING

True cloud-to-cloud lightning is rare because most lightning flashes occur within a cloud. The first lightning flash in a thunderstorm is typically an intracloud discharge. When an intracloud discharge occurs, the cloud becomes luminous for approximately 0.2 to 0.5 second. The discharge is initiated by a leader that propagates between regions of opposite charge (or from a charged region to the neutral atmosphere). Luminosity is more or less

142

continuous and has several pulses of higher luminosity of one-millisecond duration superimposed upon it. This situation suggests minor return strokes as the leader contacts pockets of opposite charge, but the similarity ends there. The total amount of the charge transfer is generally similar to the amount involved in a ground discharge: 10 coulombs, with a range from 0.3 to 100 coulombs. The mean velocity of propagation of intracloud lightning ranges from 10^4 to 10^7 metres (32,880 to 32,808,398 feet) per second. Electric currents associated with the luminous brightening are probably in the range of 1,000 to 4,000 amperes. Strikes to aircraft exhibit peak currents of only a few thousand amperes, about an order of magnitude less than currents in ground flashes—though sometimes the peak currents are large. Rise times to peak currents in

A bank of storm clouds dramatically illuminated by intracloud, as well as cloud-to-air, lightning. Chuck Doswell/Visuals Unlimited, Inc.

cloud flashes are generally slower than those in return strokes. The amount of energy dissipated by intracloud flashes is unknown.

LIGHTNING DAMAGE

Most lightning strikes cause damage through the large current flowing in the return stroke or through the heat that is generated by this and the continuing current. The precise mechanisms whereby lightning currents cause damage are not completely understood, however. If lightning strikes a person, the stroke current can damage the central nervous system, heart, lungs, and other vital organs.

When a building or power line is struck by lightning or is exposed to the intense electromagnetic fields from a nearby flash, the currents and voltages that appear on the structure are determined both by the currents and fields in the discharge and by the electrical response of the object and its grounding system. For instance, if a lightning surge enters an unprotected residence by way of an electric power line, the voltages may be large enough to cause sparks in the house wiring or appliances. When such flashovers occur, they may short-circuit the alternating current power system, and the resulting power arc may start a fire. In such instances, the lightning does not start the fire directly, but it does cause a power fault (short circuit), and then the power currents do the damage. In the case of metals, large currents heat the surface at the air-arc interface and the interior by electron collisions with the metal lattice. If this heat is also great enough, the metal will melt or evaporate.

At least three properties of the return-stroke current can cause damage: the peak current, the maximum rate of change of the initial current, and the total amount of charge transferred. For objects that have a resistive impedance, such as a ground rod or a long power line, the peak voltage during a strike is proportional to the peak current produced of the lightning stroke and the resistivity of the struck object. For example, if a 100,000 ampere peak current flows into a 10-ohm grounding system, 1 million volts will be produced. A common hazard associated with the large voltages produced by lightning strikes is the re-direction of some of the energy (that is, a flashover) from the original target to an adjacent object. Such secondary discharges, or side-flashes, often cause damage comparable to that of a direct strike, and they are one of the main hazards of standing under or near an isolated tree (or any other tall object) during a thunderstorm. Such large voltages frequently cause secondary discharges or side-flashes to radiate outward from the object that is struck to another object nearby. One form of a side-flash can even occur in the ground near the point of lightning attachment.

For objects that have an inductive electrical impedance, such as the wires in a home electrical system, the peak voltage will be proportional to the maximum rate of change of the lightning current and the inductance of the object. For example, 1 metre (3.3 feet) of straight copper wire has a self-inductance on the order of one microhenry. The peak rate of change in the lightning current in a return stroke is on the order of 100,000 amperes per microsecond. Therefore, about 100,000 volts will appear across this length of conductor for the duration of the change, typically 100 nanoseconds (billionths of a second).

The heating and subsequent burn-through of metal sheets, as on a metal roof or tank, are to a first approximation proportional to the total charge injected into the metal at the air-arc interface. Generally, large charge transfers are produced by long-duration continuing currents that are in the range of 100 to 1,000 amperes, rather than by the peak currents, which have a relatively short duration. The heat produced by long continuing currents is frequently the cause of forest fires. A typical cloud-to-ground flash transfers 20 to 30 coulombs of charge to the ground, and extreme flashes transfer hundreds and occasionally thousands of coulombs.

LIGHTNING PROTECTION

The best personal protection against lightning is to be alert to the presence of a hazard and then to take common-sense precautions, such as staying inside a house or building or inside an automobile, where one is surrounded by (but not in contact with) metal. People are advised to stay away from outside doors and windows and not to be in contact with any electrical appliances, such as a telephone, or anything connected to the plumbing system. If caught outdoors, people are advised to avoid isolated trees or other objects that are preferred targets and to keep low so as to minimize both height and contact with the ground (that is, crouch but do not lie down). Swimming pools are not safe during a lightning storm because water is a good conductor of electricity, and hence being in the pool effectively greatly multiplies the area of one's "ground" contact.

The frequency with which lightning will directly strike a building in a particular region can be estimated from the building's size and the average number of strikes that occur in the region. If a building is struck whenever a stepped leader comes within 10 metres (33 feet) of the exterior of the building, then a building that is 12 metres

(39 feet) wide and 16 metres (52 feet) long (an area of 192 square metres, or about 2,000 square feet) will have an effective strike zone of 32 metres by 36 metres (an area of 1,152 square metres, or 12,400 square feet). In a region where an average of three cloud-to-ground lightning strikes occur per square kilometre annually, such a building will experience an average of 0.0035 direct strike per year, or one strike about every 290 years (1,152 square metres [12,400 square feet] × 3 flashes per square kilometre [.39 square miles] × 10^{-6} metres [.000003 feet] per square kilometre [.39 square miles]). In a region where there is an annual average of five strikes per square kilometre, the same building will experience an average of 0.0058 direct strike per year, or one strike about every 174 years. These calculations indicate that, for the second example, an average of one of every 174 buildings of similar size will be directly struck by lightning in that region each year.

Structures may be protected from lightning by either channeling the current along the outside of the building and into the ground or by shielding the building against damage from transient currents and voltages caused by a strike. Many buildings constrain the path of lightning currents and voltages through use of lightning rods, or air terminals, and conductors that route the current down into a grounding system. When a lightning leader comes near the building, the lightning rod initiates a discharge that travels upward and connects with it, thus controlling the point of attachment of lightning to the building. A lightning rod functions only when a lightning strike in the immediate vicinity is already immanent and so does not attract significantly more lighting to the building. The down conductors and grounding system function to guide the current into the ground while minimizing damage to the structure. To minimize side-flashes, the grounding resistance should be kept as low as possible, and the geometry should be arranged so as to minimize surface breakdown. Overhead wires and grounded vertical cones may also be used to provide a cone-shaped area of lightning protection. Such systems are most efficient when their height is 30 metres (98 feet) or less.

Protection of the contents of a structure can be enhanced by using lightning arresters to reduce any transient currents and voltages that might be caused by the discharge and that might propagate into the structure as traveling waves on any electric power or telephone wires exposed to the outside environment. The most effective protection for complex structures is provided by topological shielding. This form of protection reduces amounts of voltage and power at each level of a system of successive nested shields. The partial metallic shields are isolated, and the inside surface of each is grounded to the outside surface of the next. Power surges along wires coming into the structure are deflected by arrestors, or transient protectors, to the outside surface of each shield as they travel through the series, and are thus incrementally attenuated.

Chapter 4

TORNADOES

Tornadoes are small-diameter columns of violently rotating air developed within a convective cloud and in contact with the ground. They occur most often in association with thunderstorms during the spring and summer in the mid-latitudes of both the Northern and Southern Hemispheres. These whirling atmospheric vortices can generate the strongest winds known on Earth: wind speeds in the range of 500 kilometres (300 miles) per hour have been measured in extreme events. When winds of this magnitude strike a populated area, they can cause fantastic destruction and great loss of life, mainly through injuries from flying debris and collapsing structures. Most tornadoes, however, are comparatively weak events that occur in sparsely populated areas and cause minor damage.

THE PHYSICAL CHARACTERISTICS OF TORNADOES

Tornadoes are characterized by separate airflow regions, high windspeeds, and low atmospheric pressure. In addition, they are easily recognized by their funnel-shaped clouds, where Earth's strongest surficial winds manifest themselves.

AIRFLOW REGIONS

Fully developed tornadoes contain distinct regions of airflow. The central axis of circulation is within the core region, a roughly cylindrical area of lower atmospheric pressure that is bounded by the maximum tangential winds (the fastest winds circulating around the centre of the tornado). If a visible funnel cloud forms, it will occur within the core region. The funnel cloud consists of a column of water droplets, commonly called the condensation funnel. In very dry conditions there may be no condensation funnel associated with a tornado.

Responding to the reduced pressure in the central core, air near the ground located in what is referred to as the inflow boundary layer converges from all directions into a tornado's "corner region." This region gets its name because the wind abruptly "turns the corner" from primarily horizontal to vertical flow as it enters the core region and begins its upward spiral. The corner region is very violent. It is often marked by a dust whirl or a debris fountain, where the erupting inflow carries aloft material ripped from the surface. The inflow boundary layer that feeds the corner region is usually a few tens of metres deep and has turbulent airflow. Above the boundary layer, the core is surrounded by a weakly swirling outer flow—the inflow to the storm's updraft—where radial motions (movements toward or away from the tornado's axis) are relatively small. Somewhere aloft (exactly where is not known), the core and the swirling outer flow merge with the updraft of the generating thunderstorm.

Winds in a tornado are almost always cyclonic; that is, they turn counterclockwise in the Northern Hemisphere and clockwise in the Southern Hemisphere. This dominance of rotation direction is indirectly due to the Earth's rotation, which plays a role in controlling the structure of all large-scale weather systems. As is explained more fully in the section Tornado Formation, most tornadoes are produced by thunderstorms, and a tornado's parent thunderstorm is in turn embedded within a larger weather system that determines the vertical shear in the winds (that is, their change in speed and direction with height across the troposphere). These systems rotate cyclonically, and a tornado's rotation comes from a concentration of the spin present in the sheared winds. However, not all tornadoes are cyclonic. About 5 percent of all observed tornadoes rotate anticyclonically—that is, they turn clockwise in the Northern Hemisphere and counterclockwise in the Southern Hemisphere.

WIND SPEEDS AND AIR PRESSURES

Measurement of wind speeds can be obtained by photogrammetry (measurements from photographs) and through remote sensing techniques using the Doppler effect. These two techniques are complementary. They provide information about tornado wind speeds by tracking objects in and around the core (the assumption being that the objects are moving with the speed of the air). Photogrammetry allows speeds across the image plane to be determined by analysis of motions of dust packets, pieces of vegetation, and building debris as recorded on film or videotape, but it cannot be used to determine wind speed toward or away from the camera. On the other hand, through processing of Doppler-shifted electromagnetic "echoes" received from raindrops and debris illuminated with pulses of radio waves (radar) or light (lidar), wind speed toward or away from the instrument can be determined.

Under some conditions, extreme wind speeds can occur in the corner region of a tornado. The few measurements of violent tornado winds that have been made using Doppler radar and photogrammetry suggest that the maximum possible tangential wind speeds generated by tornadoes are in the range of 125 to 160 metres per second, or 450 to 575 kilometres per hour (about 410 to 525 feet per second, or 280 to 360 miles per hour). Most researchers believe the actual extreme value is near the lower end of this range. Consistent with this thinking was the measurement made using a mobile Doppler radar of the fastest wind speed ever measured, 318 miles per hour (about 512 kilometres per hour), in a tornado that hit the suburbs of Oklahoma City, Oklahoma, on May 3, 1999.

Maximum tangential speeds occur in a ring-shaped region that surrounds the tip of the vortex core that is centred 30 to 50 metres (100 to 160 feet) above the ground. (Hence, they tend to be a bit higher than damage-causing winds at the surface.) The vertical speeds of air rising as a central jet through the hole in the ring may be as high as 80 metres per second, or 300 kilometres per hour (about 250 feet per second, or 170 miles per hour). Radial speeds of air flowing from the inflow region to the corner region (which feeds the central jet) are estimated to reach 50 metres per second, or 180 kilometres per hour (about 160 feet per second, or 110 miles per hour). Because the organization of the airflow varies considerably with tornado intensity, extremes in vertical and radial speeds may not occur at the same time as extremes in tangential speeds.

These extreme speeds are the strongest winds known to occur near the Earth's surface. In reality, they occur over a very small portion of the tornado core close to the ground. Their actual occurrence is rare, and, when they do occur, they usually last only a very short time. In almost all tornadoes (about 98 percent), the maximum attained wind speed is much less than these maximum possible speeds.

While there have not been any direct measurements of atmospheric pressure in tornadoes, a few measurements have been taken when tornadoes passed near weather stations with barographs (instruments that record atmospheric pressure over time). Data from such incidents, along with measurements made in laboratory vortices, provide for the construction of mathematical models describing the distribution of surface pressure beneath tornadoes. These models, combined with information on tornado winds, are used to extrapolate what was the most likely air pressure at the centre of any given tornado.

These extrapolations indicate that a region of low surface pressure is centred beneath the tornado core. The area of this region is relatively small compared with that of the annulus of high-speed winds that surrounds it. Even for violent tornadoes, the reduction in surface pressure in this area (relative to surface pressure in the surrounding atmosphere) is probably no more than 100 hectopascals (that is, about 10 percent of standard atmospheric pressure at sea level). In most tornadoes, the reduction in central surface pressure is not that great.

The lowest atmospheric pressure in a tornado is thought to be at the centre of the core a few tens to a few hundred metres (feet) above the surface, though the magnitude of the pressure reduction is unknown. In violent tornadoes this pressure difference appears to be sufficient to induce a central downflow.

FUNNEL CLOUDS

A tornado is often made visible by a distinctive funnel-shaped cloud. Commonly called the condensation funnel, the funnel cloud is a tapered column of water droplets that extends downward from the base of the parent cloud. It is commonly mixed with and perhaps enveloped by dust and debris lifted from the surface. The funnel cloud may be present but not visible due to heavy rain. Over a tornado's lifetime, the size and shape of the funnel cloud may change markedly, reflecting changes in the intensity of the winds, the moisture content of the inflowing air, properties of the ground, and other factors. Very frequently the condensation funnel extends from the parent cloud only partway to the ground, and in very dry conditions there may be no condensation funnel. Generally, the more moist the air and the more intense the tornado, the larger the funnel cloud.

Caption: A mesocyclone tornado exhibiting the familiar funnel shape associated with tornadoes. Funnel clouds are comprised of swirling water droplets mixed with dust and debris. National Oceanic and Atmospheric Administration/Department of Commerce. OAR/ERL/National Severe Storms Laboratory

The funnel cloud usually outlines only the innermost core. Typically, its diameter is at most one-tenth that of the overall tornado circulation. Indeed, a tornado can occur without a funnel cloud being present at all. The funnel cloud's length can range from tens of metres to several kilometres. Its diameter can span a few metres to hundreds of metres. Funnel clouds of weak tornadoes are usually cone-shaped, while strong and violent tornadoes form short, broad, cylindrical pillars. Long, rope-like tubes that trail off horizontally are common in the waning phase of many tornadoes.

DURATION

The lifetime of a tornado is directly related to its intensity, with more intense tornadoes tending to last longer. On average, a tornado is on the ground for about 15 minutes, but this value is misleading because the average is heavily weighted by the rare but long-lived violent tornadoes. Most tornadoes are weak, lasting only about two to three minutes on average. A typical lifetime for strong tornadoes is about 8 minutes, while for violent events it is about 25 minutes. In exceptional cases, violent events can last more than three hours.

THE SPEED AND DIRECTION OF MOVEMENT

The movement of a tornado is determined by the motion of the generating thunderstorm. The average tornado moves at a speed of about 12 to 13 metres per second, or 43 to 47 kilometres per hour (about 39 to 43 feet per second, or 27 to 29 miles per hour), but some have remained nearly stationary while others have traveled faster than 25 metres per second, or 90 kilometres per hour (80 feet per second, or 55 miles per hour). As an extreme example, speeds of up to 33 metres per second, or 120 kilometres per hour (110 feet per second, or 75 miles per hour) were measured in a tornado that struck Guin, Alabama, on April 3, 1974.

Most tornado-producing thunderstorms occur in a warm air mass that is under the influence of an active synoptic-scale low-pressure system (such a system covers about one-half of the continent). The middle-level winds (3 to 10 kilometres [2 to 6 miles] in altitude) that in large part determine the direction of storm motion tend to be from the west or southwest in the Northern Hemisphere. Hence, most tornadoes (around 80 percent) come from the west or southwest and move to the east or northeast. Tornadoes move from northwest to southeast about 5 percent of the time. Many hurricane-related tornadoes have traveled east to west, as have a few Great Plains and Midwest tornadoes. In the Southern Hemisphere, storms (and consequently tornadoes) tend to move from the west or northwest to the east or southeast.

Tornado Cyclones, Tornado Families, and Long-Track Tornadoes

About 90 percent of tornadoes are associated with thunderstorms, usually supercells. This association accounts for many weak and almost all strong and violent tornadoes. The other 10 percent of tornado occurrences are associated with rapidly growing cumulus clouds. These vortices are almost always weak and short-lived.

As a very rough estimate, about 100,000 thunderstorms occur in the United States each year. About 10 percent of these (or about 10,000 per year) will become severe thunderstorms, and only about 5 percent to 10 percent of these severe storms (or about 500 to 1,000 per year) will produce tornadoes.

The typical tornado-producing thunderstorm lasts for two to three hours and usually produces one or two relatively short-lived tornadoes. The period of storm maturity during which a tornado is most likely to form may last only a few tens of minutes. However, on rare occasions a storm may produce a tornado cyclone (a core of concentrated rotation within the storm from which tornadoes are spawned) that is stable and long-lived. The strength of the tornado cyclone usually pulsates, creating a sequence of tornadoes. This gives rise to what is known as a tornado family. Tornado families typically have two or three members, though they can be much larger. During the Super Outbreak of April 3–4, 1974, in the United States, a single storm traveling along the Ohio River produced a family with eight members spread over several hundred kilometres.

On very rare occasions, the strength of a tornado cyclone will remain nearly constant for several hours, forming a single, long-lasting tornado with a continuous damage path many times the average length. This is referred to as a long-track tornado. Long-track tornadoes can be difficult to distinguish from tornado families. For instance, the Great Tri-State Tornado of March 18, 1925, is credited with a path length of 352 kilometres (219 miles), though it cannot be proved that this event, which affected Missouri, Illinois, and Indiana, was an individual tornado or a series in the same family. On the other hand, the Monticello, Indiana, tornado on April 3, 1974 (part of the Super Outbreak mentioned above), produced a continuous track of damage for over 160 kilometres (99 miles). It was also the fifth and final member of a tornado family.

TORNADO FORMATION

Tornadoes may occur wherever conditions favour the development of strong thunderstorms. Essential conditions for such storms are the presence of cool, dry air at middle levels in the troposphere, overlying a layer of moist, conditionally unstable air near the surface of the Earth. Conditional instability occurs when a saturated air parcel (air at 100 percent relative humidity) continues to rise once set in motion, but an unsaturated air parcel resists being displaced vertically. The unsaturated air, if moved upward, will be cooler than the surrounding air and it will sink. On the other hand, when conditionally unstable air rises it becomes warmer owing to the condensation of water vapour. As the water condenses, heat is released, further warming the air and fueling its rise. This convective action (that is, the circulation of air as a result of heat transfer) produces the huge clouds commonly associated with thunderstorms and tornadoes. Convection can be initiated when the Sun heats a localized area of the ground, destabilizing the near-surface air.

Thunderstorms can also form along the boundary, or front, between air masses of different temperatures. In this case, the denser cool air displaces the warmer and forces it to rise. The greater the contrast in temperature and moisture across the frontal boundary, the greater the instability of the atmosphere and the greater the likelihood of a strong thunderstorm.

Most tornadoes are formed when a strong updraft such as those described above acts to concentrate atmospheric rotation, or spin, into a swirling column of air. Spin is a natural occurrence in air because horizontal winds almost always experience both an increase in speed and a veering in direction with increasing height above the surface. The increase of wind speed with height (called vertical speed shear) produces "crosswise spin," that is, rotation about a horizontal axis crosswise to the direction of wind flow. When air containing crosswise spin flows into an updraft, the spin is drawn upward, producing rotation about a vertical axis. The veering of wind direction with height (vertical direction shear) is another source of horizontal spin, this time oriented in the same direction as the wind flow and known as "streamwise spin." When air containing streamwise spin is drawn into an updraft, it too is tilted upward and rotates about a vertical axis. Although crosswise spin and streamwise spin are oriented at right angles to each other, both rotations exist in the horizontal plane, and both types have been revealed by Doppler radar observations to contribute to the evolution of a rotating updraft. Radar observations also have shown that updraft rotation makes its appearance in a thunderstorm at altitudes of 4 to 8 kilometres (2.5 to 5 miles). At first, the tilting of crosswise spin into the vertical appears to be the principal mechanism of rotation. Subsequently, as updraft rotation intensifies, the tilting of streamwise spin becomes more important. The resulting swirling column of rising air, perhaps 10 to 20 kilometres (6 to 12 miles) in diameter and only weakly rotating, is called a mesocyclone.

THE DYNAMIC PIPE

As spin-up of the mesocyclone continues, its rotating action begins to reorganize airflow in the updraft. The local pressure field and the strongly curved wind field move toward a dynamic equilibrium called cyclostrophic balance. In this state, the pressure-gradient force, which acts to move air inward in response to the lower pressure in the centre of the rotating column, is equaled by the outward-directed centrifugal force. When cyclostrophic balance is achieved, air readily flows in a circular path around the mesocyclone's axis, while flow toward or away from its centre is strongly suppressed. This state, in which airflow is constrained by its own rotation, is known as the dynamic pipe effect.

The middle level of the storm is usually the first area where cyclostrophic balance is achieved, and it is this section of the mesocyclone that begins to act as a dynamic pipe. Almost all the air flowing along the mesocyclone's axis is drawn in through the bottom of the pipe. This inflow further intensifies rotation at the pipe's lower end, causing it to extend rapidly downward as the more quickly rotating region comes into cyclostrophic balance.

Strong convergence of inflowing air at the lower end of the pipe causes air parcels to be accelerated upward and

This diagram illustrates tornado formation. The difference in speeds and temperatures of the air currents has a significant impact on the strength of a tornado. Gary Hincks/Photo Researchers, Inc.

vertically "stretched." Vertical stretching normally causes the mesocyclone to contract to a diameter of about 2 to 6 kilometres (1 to 4 miles). As this happens, the mesocyclone rotates more quickly, which in turn strengthens the convergence of inflowing winds at its base. In this manner the mesocyclone grows in strength in a positive-feedback, or self-amplifying, process.

Development of the dynamic pipe effect can produce a mesocyclone that extends the full depth of the thunderstorm, from about 1 kilometre (0.6 mile) above the ground to near the storm's top at about 15 kilometres (9 miles). Frequently, the maturation of the mesocyclone is heralded at the bottom of the cloud by a lowering of a portion of the thunderstorm's base in the area of the updraft. This approximately cylindrical extension is known as a wall cloud. Surface winds with speeds as high as 33 metres per second, or 120 kilometres per hour (110 feet per second, or 75 miles per hour) can be present beneath this swirling cloud, often producing damage even when no tornado forms.

THE TORNADO CORE AND THE CONDENSATION FUNNEL

The extension of a concentrated swirling core to the surface—in other words, the actual formation of a tornado—can occur once the mesocyclone is established. Most mesocyclones do not generate tornadoes. In the ones that do, a small region of increased convergence and stretching that is typically no more than 1 kilometre (.6 mile) in diameter develops in the mesocyclone for reasons that have so far eluded storm researchers. This usually occurs at the interface between the thunderstorm's updraft and downdraft. Enhanced spin begins several kilometres (miles) above the ground, then quickly builds downward. Around such a small volume, rotation is strong enough for a smaller dynamic pipe to form and extend to within several tens of metres of the surface. This dynamic pipe is called the tornado core. Once it forms, the parent mesocyclone is reclassified as a tornado cyclone.

As the core approaches the ground, surface friction slows the rotational motion and prevents the establishment of cyclostrophic balance. Surface friction also limits the rate of airflow into the base of the core. This restriction prevents inflow from filling the tornado's low-pressure core from below. At the same time, the parent storm's strong updraft prevents sufficient air from filling the core from above.

With air pressure in the vortex core thus reduced in comparison to the pressure outside the core at the same elevation, a condensation funnel forms. This occurs because, at lower atmospheric pressure, air flowing upward in the core cools more quickly with increasing height than air rising at higher pressure just outside the core. Assuming that inflowing air has the same amount of moisture throughout, air rising in the core reaches its dew point at a lower height than air rising just outside the core. Any further rise leads to condensation and a visible cloud. Because pressure is lowest at the axis of the vortex, air rising along this centre line reaches its dew point nearer the ground than air spiraling up just a short distance outward. This process gives rise to the characteristic conical or funnel shape of the condensation cloud.

THE LOCATION IN THE PARENT STORM

Many weak tornadoes form between the surface and the lowest portion of the parent cloud. These tornadoes exist for only a short time (a few minutes). Such tornadoes most commonly form beneath the flanking line of cumulus congestus clouds that frequently develop above a strong thunderstorm's gust front (the leading edge of the storm's downdraft). Often called gustnadoes, these vortices are true tornadoes when they are attached to the updraft of a rapidly growing congestus cloud. Gustnadoes draw their spin from the wind shear across the gust front. Their transient nature, relatively small diameters, and lack of a rotating region within the generating cloud cause them to be difficult to observe with radar. As a result, small tornadoes are not well documented, and in many respects they are less understood than stronger events.

In contrast to gustnadoes, almost all strong and violent tornadoes (and some weak ones as well) are closely connected with a rotating updraft that extends through much of the height of the parent storm. Such tornadoes tend to form near the interface between a storm's updraft and downdraft. To an observer on the ground, they are generally perceived as being beneath the right-rear quadrant of the main body of the storm in the Northern Hemisphere as viewed along the storm path. Because of the connection of these tornadoes to large-diameter circulations within the thunderstorm, many of the events leading to their formation have been fairly well documented both visually and by radar.

TORNADO INTENSITY

Understanding how tornadoes form only tells part of the story. Scientists also need to understand how strong or intense tornadoes can be and what factors lead to these different intensities. Tornado intensity is not estimated directly from measured wind speeds, because tornadoes rarely pass near meteorological instruments. Rather, it is commonly estimated by analyzing damage to structures and then correlating that damage with the wind speeds required to produce such destruction. This method is essential to assigning tornadoes specific values on the Enhanced Fujita Scale, or EF-Scale, of tornado intensity. The notion of developing such a scale for use in comparing events and in research was proposed in 1971 by the Japanese American meteorologist T. Theodore Fujita.

Fujita's scale was widely used in the United States and adapted for use in other parts of the world. However, almost from the beginning, the limitations of his approach were recognized. The primary criticisms were a lack of sufficient damage indicators for the many building types found in modern society, no recognition of regional variations in types and quality of construction of otherwise similar structures, and a lack of a definitive correlation between observed damage and wind speed. As a result, there were inconsistencies in the rating of tornado intensity in the historical records (which is shown as noise in statistical analyses). Also, tornado wind speeds, especially in very high wind events, were overestimated.

In 2004, after 33 years of experience with the original Fujita Scale, leading atmospheric researchers and tornado forecasters developed a plan to improve the estimation process and eliminate some of the limitations. The result, the Enhanced Fujita Scale, was adopted for use in 2007. It retains many of the features of the original scale but provides more precision at the higher intensity values. The scientists and forecasters also worked out ways to adjust the older records so that EF values would be available for the comparison.

To classify a tornado using the EF-Scale, the damage occurring along the tornado's track is mapped. A tornado's intensity varies along its path, with the most extreme damage usually being restricted to a small area, and the overall EF-Scale value assigned represents the tornado's highest attained intensity. Once the degree of damage to structures and vegetation has been assessed and matched with the appropriate EF-Scale value, the maximum wind velocities within the range associated with the EF-Scale value are assigned. Even in its improved form, such a system is inevitably limited. For example, a powerful tornado that does not pass near buildings or trees, causing little or no damage, may be given an EF-Scale value less than its true intensity.

The Enhanced Fujita Scale recognizes tornadoes of six different intensities ranging in number from EF0 to EF5. For many purposes, these can be grouped into three broader categories—weak, strong, and violent—which are described in turn below, using Fujita's original photographs to illustrate the type of damage associated with each category.

WEAK (EF0 AND EF1) TORNADOES

Though most tornadoes (60 to 70 percent) are in this category, they account for less than 5 percent of all deaths. A weak tornado usually has a single funnel cloud (that is, a column of water droplets) resembling an elongated, upward-opening cone with a smooth surface. The cone often does not touch the ground. In weak tornadoes, vertical wind speeds are thought to be greatest along the central axis of circulation. Many weak tornadoes appear not to extend upward far beyond the base of the parent storm.

STRONG (EF2 AND EF3) TORNADOES

About 35 percent of all tornadoes are in the strong category, and they account for about 30 percent of all deaths. Typically, a strong tornado has a broad, columnar funnel cloud. The funnel surface usually has a rough, rapidly changing texture, reflecting small-scale turbulence. Available evidence suggests that in a strong tornado, most of the rising air surges upward in a cylindrical annulus around the central axis. Vertical speeds are lower along the axis itself. Sometimes "suction vortices" can be seen within the tornado core at its point of contact with the ground. This little-understood feature appears to contain the highest wind speeds in the tornado. Strong tornadoes extend well up into the generating thunderstorm because they generally form in or around a strongly rotating updraft that may persist through the storm's full height.

VIOLENT (EF4 AND EF5) TORNADOES

Only a very few tornadoes (2 percent or so) reach intensities high enough to be categorized as violent. However, they account for about 65 percent of all deaths. In many cases, a violent tornado has a broad core with a diameter of 0.5 kilometres (0.3 mile) or more. At the centre of the core, there is a relatively calm and clear eye. In the eye, nonswirling air flows down from upper levels of the thunderstorm due to low pressure in the base of the core. Upon reaching the ground, this descending inner flow turns outward and mixes with air rushing in from the inflow boundary layer (that is, the layer of air near ground level). The combined flow then spirals upward around the eye in an annulus.

In some violent tornadoes, secondary vortices may form in the annulus, giving rise to what is termed a multiple-vortex tornado. In these secondary vortices, air spins rapidly around the axes while the vortices themselves rotate around the periphery of the central eye. Small secondary vortices are also called suction vortices when they are most evident in the corner region, the area where the wind entering the base of the tornado abruptly "turns the corner" from primarily horizontal to vertical flow. A tornado with one or more suction vortices is distinguished from a multiple-vortex tornado in that a suction vortex is at most only several hundreds of metres (feet) high, while multiple vortices extend all the way up into the cloud base of the parent thunderstorm. The fastest known surface winds occur around the tips of secondary vortices.

TORNADO OCCURRENCE AND DISTRIBUTION

Although tornadoes are sighted throughout the world, the overwhelming majority occur in North America. The United States, specifically the state of Texas, is the site of the most tornadoes. However, tornadoes may also occur in various Midwestern states throughout the year.

THE OCCURRENCE OF TORNADOES AROUND THE GLOBE

Tornadoes have been reported on all continents except Antarctica. They are most common on continents in the mid-latitudes (between 20° and 60° N and S), where they are frequently associated with thunderstorms that develop in regions where cold polar air meets warm tropical air.

Calculating which country has the most tornadoes per year depends on how this measurement is defined. The United Kingdom has the most tornadoes per land size, most of them weak. On average, about 33 tornadoes are reported annually there. In absolute numbers, the United States has the most tornadoes by far (more than 1,000 per year have been reported every year since 1990).

It also has the most violent tornadoes (about 10 to 20 per year). Tornadoes of this intensity are very infrequent outside of the United States. Canada reports the second largest number of tornadoes (about 80 to 100 annually). Russia may have many tornadoes, but reports are not available to quantify their occurrence. About 20 tornadoes are reported in Australia each year, though the actual number is likely much higher. Many storms occur in uninhabited areas, and so any tornadoes that they produce are undocumented.

Records of tornado occurrences are fragmentary for many areas, making estimates of global tornado frequency difficult. Insurance records show that tornadoes have caused significant losses in Europe, India, Japan, South Africa, and Australia. Rare but deadly tornadoes have occurred in many other countries, including Bangladesh, China, and Argentina. There are few tornado reports from either the Arctic or the equatorial tropics.

In the United Kingdom almost all reported tornadoes are associated with vigorous convection occurring in advance of and along a cold frontal boundary. Large temperature differences are associated with early winter cold fronts that move rapidly across the country from the north and west, at times spawning widespread outbreaks of small tornadoes. For example, the passage of a very strong frontal boundary across the United Kingdom on Nov. 23, 1981, produced 105 documented tornadoes. Similar phenomena occur in other European countries such as France and Belgium.

Most Southern Hemisphere tornadoes occur in Australia. Many reports come from New South Wales, where there were 173 reported tornadoes from 1901 to 1966. In addition, South Africa and Argentina both reported 191 tornadoes from 1930 to 1979. Because tornado formation is closely tied to the speed and directional shear of the wind with height, tornadoes in the Southern Hemisphere almost exclusively rotate clockwise, opposite to the rotation of their Northern Hemisphere counterparts.

TORNADO OCCURRENCE IN THE UNITED STATES

Though tornadoes occur in every state, they are most frequent and attain the highest intensities in the central portion of the United States. Texas has the most reported tornadoes each year, about 125 on average for the years 1953–91. Florida, with almost 10 tornadoes per 10,000 square miles (26,000 square kilometres) per year, has the most per area. However, most Florida tornadoes are very weak and affect extremely small areas.

From 1916 through 1998, about 45,000 tornadoes were documented in the United States. From 1916 to 1953, approximately 158 tornadoes were reported per year. After 1953, the beginning of the "modern period" of tornado documentation, the number of reports rose to more than 800 per year. (The modern period is considered to have begun in 1953 because this was the first full year in which the U.S. Weather Bureau issued tornado watches—that is, bulletins reporting that a tornado might be imminent.) The increased number of tornadoes reported was due to improvements in observing and recording (largely because of the establishment of a network of volunteer tornado "spotters"), which allowed a greater number of weak events to be recognized. During the interval from 1953 to 1998, there was an average of 169 "tornado days" (days on which one or more tornadoes were reported) per year. However, the early years of the modern period, with their relatively fewer reports, bias these averages. If only the 15 years from 1984 through 1998 were considered, the average number of tornadoes per year would be 1,025, occurring on 173 tornado days per year. These higher numbers are attributed to additional improvements in tornado reporting.

THE GEOGRAPHIC DISTRIBUTION OF TORNADOES

When the number of tornado occurrences, their intensity, and the area they affect are considered, the centre of tornado activity is unquestionably seen to exist in the western portions of the southern Great Plains. The region of maximum tornado frequency, rightfully called Tornado Alley, extends from west Texas northeast through the western and central portions of Oklahoma and Kansas and across most of Nebraska.

Another area of frequent tornado occurrence is found across eastern Iowa, Illinois, Indiana, western Ohio, the southern portions of Wisconsin and Michigan, and the northern part of Kentucky. While this area experiences fewer tornadoes than does Tornado Alley, it has been struck by some of the strongest known tornadoes and has been the site of several large tornado outbreaks (that is, the occurrence of multiple tornadoes from the same weather system). The Gulf states (from east Texas to central Florida) have many weak tornadoes and have had outbreaks. The Gulf states also experience many tornadoes associated with hurricanes.

SEASONAL PATTERNS

While most tornadoes develop in the spring and summer, tornadoes have occurred every day of the year. Several days have had many occurrences, reflecting large regional and national outbreaks. The distribution of reported tornadoes by month for the period 1916 through 1990 shows that about 74 percent of all tornadoes are reported from

March through July. Peak months are April (14 percent), May (22 percent), and June (20 percent). December and January are the months of lowest activity.

The main concentration of tornado activity migrates across the central portion of the United States in a seasonal cycle. Toward the end of winter (late February), the centre of tornado activity lies over the central Gulf states. At this time, southward-moving cold air reaches the southern limit of its expansion and encroaches on the Gulf Coast. As spring progresses, the days grow longer and more solar energy is intercepted. Land temperatures rise, and warm, moist air from the Gulf of Mexico progressively drives back the cold air. The centre of activity then moves eastward to the southeastern Atlantic states, with tornado frequency peaking there in April.

As spring advances and gives way to summer, the centre of tornado activity gradually shifts westward and then northward. It moves across the southern Plains in May and June and then into the northern Plains and the Great Lakes states by early summer. Late summer through early fall is usually a relatively quiet time because the temperature and moisture contrasts across the boundary between the two air masses are weak. An extension of the Bermuda high (a centre of high atmospheric pressure that develops over the Atlantic Ocean) dominates the southeastern third of the United States, and, while thunderstorms occur frequently in the warm, moist air, they seldom become severe. In late fall the days grow shorter, the temperature and moisture contrast intensifies again, and the centre of tornado activity retreats south toward the Gulf, completing the annual cycle.

Superimposed on this general pattern are large year-to-year variations. These arise because almost all tornado-producing storms are embedded within episodic northward surges of warm, moist air. The distribution of tornadoes in any one year thus reflects the weather patterns—especially the tracks followed by the synoptic-scale low-pressure centres—prevailing in that year.

Regional factors must also be taken into account. Along the Gulf Coast, tornadoes can be produced by thunderstorms that come ashore as a hurricane makes landfall. In a few cases, many tornadoes will be produced. For example, on Sept. 20, 1967, thunderstorms in Hurricane Beulah produced 115 tornadoes in south Texas.

DIURNAL PATTERNS

Although tornadoes can occur at all times of the day, they are most frequent from mid-afternoon to early evening. In the central United States, where most tornadoes occur, tornado frequency is highest between 5:00 and 6:00 PM. Weak and strong tornadoes occur most frequently in this same hour. Violent tornado occurrences peak an hour later, between 6:00 and 7:00 PM. Tornado occurrences peak in the late afternoon to early evening because there must be sufficient time for the Sun strongly to heat the ground and the surface layer of the atmosphere, thus inducing and sustaining severe thunderstorms. Few reports (roughly 1 percent) are from between 5:00 and 6:00 AM, the period just around sunrise when the atmosphere is often very stable.

TORNADO OUTBREAKS

A tornado outbreak is the occurrence of several tornadoes over a region, usually due to thunderstorms embedded in the same synoptic-scale weather system. Outbreaks are classified according to the number of tornadoes reported: small (6 to 9 tornadoes), medium (10 to 19), and large (more than 20 tornadoes). Outbreaks are also classified according to the area affected: in local outbreaks, one or only a portion of one state is affected; in regional outbreaks, two or three states contain all or almost all the tornadoes; in national outbreaks, tornadoes are reported in many states.

On most tornado days, only a relatively small region has the essential conditions juxtaposed in just the right way to foster tornado development. This alignment usually lasts for only a small portion of an afternoon. As a consequence, only the two or three storms that form in this region are likely to produce tornadoes. Most of these vortices are weak, but one or more may be strong. Most occur in the space of one to two hours in the middle to late afternoon. Situations like this give rise to small local outbreaks several times per year.

Most dangerous are national outbreaks. Perhaps once every 10 to 15 years, the synoptic-scale weather pattern produces conditions favourable to the production of strong storms over a large portion of the central United States. The number of conditions required to align over this large an area usually limits the occurrence of such widespread outbreaks to March and April. Many of the tornadoes are likely to be strong or violent. The largest national tornado outbreak was the Super Outbreak of April 3–4, 1974, which was credited with producing 148 tornadoes in the central and southern United States (though 4 of these were later reclassified as downbursts by the meteorologist T. Theodore Fujita). The second largest was the April 11–12, 1965, Palm Sunday Outbreak.

THE PREDICTION AND DETECTION OF TORNADOES

The first step in predicting the likely occurrence of tornadoes involves identifying regions where conditions are favourable to the development of strong thunderstorms. Essential ingredients for the occurrence of such storms are cool, dry air at middle levels in the troposphere superimposed over a layer of moist, conditionally unstable air near the surface.

Conditions commonly leading to thunderstorm development occur along the warm side of the boundary line, or front, that separates cold, dry air from warm, moist air. The degree of instability present in the atmosphere is approximated by the contrasts in temperature and moisture across the frontal boundary that divides the two air masses. For a storm to generate tornadoes, other factors must be present. The most important of these is a veering wind profile (that is, a progressive shifting of the wind, clockwise in the Northern Hemisphere, counterclockwise in the Southern Hemisphere, with increasing height) at low and middle levels, along with strong winds at high levels. Both of these wind actions are necessary to provide the required spin in the air that may eventually culminate in a tornado. A veering wind profile can be provided by the same strong temperature contrasts powering the thunderstorm, and high-altitude winds can be provided by the jet stream, the thin ribbon of high-speed air found in the upper half of the troposphere.

For the generation of a tornado, the diffuse spin must be concentrated into a small area as an evolving storm goes through several distinct stages of development. The first appearance of rotation in a storm is caused by the interaction of a strong, persistent updraft with the winds that blow through and around the storm. Rotation intensifies as the speed of the wind increases and as its direction veers from southeast to south and then around to west (in the Northern Hemisphere) with increasing height through the lower half of the troposphere.

Forecasters in the United States have learned to carefully monitor the wind profile in regions of instability and to estimate how temperatures and winds will evolve through the course of a day, while at the same time tracking the movement and intensity of the jet stream. With the aid of modern observing systems, such as vertically pointing radars (called wind profilers) and imaging systems on satellites that can measure the flow of water vapour through the Earth's atmosphere, forecasters can usually identify where conditions will be favourable for tornado formation one to seven hours in advance. This information is transmitted to the public as a tornado watch. A tornado warning is issued when a tornado has been spotted either visually or on a weather radar.

Once strong thunderstorms begin to form, local offices of the National Weather Service monitor their development using imagery from satellite sensors and, most important, from radars. These allow forecasters to follow the evolution of the storms and to estimate their intensity. In the past, weather surveillance radars provided information only on the intensity of rainfall within the storms. Weather forecasters then had to infer the onset of rotation within a storm's updraft from circumstantial evidence, such as when the precipitation began to curve around the updraft to produce a "hook echo," a hook-shaped region of precipitation that flows out of the main storm and wraps around the updraft. Such inferences were highly subjective and prone to false alarms or very short-notice warnings. Today, modern weather surveillance radars not only provide information on the intensity of a storm's rainfall but also utilize the Doppler principle to sense winds within thunderstorms. Wind speeds are determined from radio waves reflected by raindrops and other particles carried along by the wind.

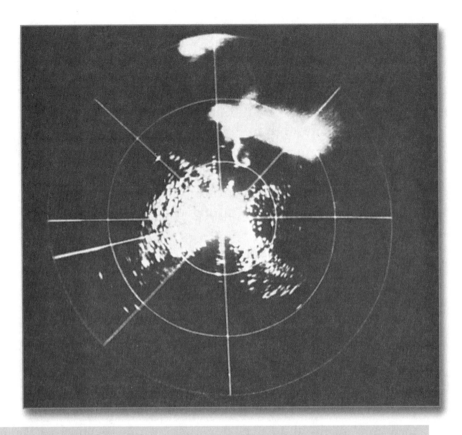

Hook echo of a tornado in Champaign, Ill., photographed on a radar scope on April 9, 1953. This was the first occasion on which the hook echo, an important clue in the tornado warning system, was recorded. Courtesy of the Illinois State Water Survey, Champaign, Illinois; photograph, Donald W. Staggs

Doppler radars can measure rotation in the updraft and allow forecasters to watch the formation of a mesocyclone (that is, a region of rotating air within a thunderstorm). On Doppler radar, the presence of a well-organized mesocyclone is indicated by a small region of concentrated shear in the wind. On one side of the mesocyclone the rotating winds flow toward the radar; and on the other, they move away. In some cases, the formation of the tornado core can be detected. The tornado core is a roughly cylindrical region of lower atmospheric pressure that is bounded by the maximum tangential winds (the fastest winds circulating around the centre of the tornado). The radar indication of intense concentrated rotation is called the tornado vortex signature, although this area does not always evolve into a tornado core. These improvements have allowed forecasters to increase warning times while reducing false alarms.

Death and Damage

In the period 1916 through 1998, tornadoes claimed 12,282 lives in the United States, an average of 150 deaths per year. For the period 1953 through 1998, tornadoes claimed 4,032 lives, an average of 88 deaths per year. The decrease in fatalities is due to improvements in safety awareness and severe-weather warnings. There have been wide variations in the number of deaths from one year to the next, the minimum being 15 deaths in 1986 and the maximum being 805 in 1925 (due largely to the Great Tri-State Tornado of March 18, 1925). Since the advent of improved warning systems, three years contributed disproportionately to the total number of deaths: 1953, 1965, and 1974. Of the 519 deaths in 1953, 323 were due to strong tornadoes striking three urban areas (Waco, Texas; Flint, Michigan; and Worcester, Massachusetts). The high death counts in 1965 and 1974 (301 and 366, respectively) were the result of large national tornado outbreaks—the April 11–12, 1965, Palm Sunday Outbreak and the greatest of all recorded outbreaks, the April 3–4, 1974, Super Outbreak.

Most deaths and injuries in tornadoes result from individuals being struck by flying debris. People are sometimes injured or killed by being rolled across the ground by the high winds. Also, a few people appear to have been killed by being carried aloft and then dropped from a great height.

Almost all of the damage caused by tornadoes can be attributed to wind-induced forces tearing structures apart. High-speed air flowing over a building's roof and around its corners produces forces that pull upward and outward, respectively. Once windows or doors on the windward side of a building break, air rushes in, pushing outward on the remaining walls and upward on the roof from the inside, and adding to the forces induced by the outside airflow. Often a building is torn apart so quickly and dramatically by these forces that it appears to explode.

It used to be thought that many buildings "exploded" owing to the development of an extreme difference in pressure between their interiors and the outside air. The rate at which pressure changes at a point on the surface as a tornado approaches may be as great as 100 hectopascals per second (100 hectopascals are equivalent to about 10 percent of atmospheric pressure at sea level). While this is a significant drop, studies have shown that most structures are sufficiently open that, even with the high rate of pressure change associated with a rapidly moving tornado, interior pressure can adjust quickly enough to prevent an explosion. Indeed, since the area of greatly reduced pressure beneath a tornado is small compared with the area of damaging winds, it is likely that a building already will have suffered damage from the winds by the time it experiences a rapid drop in outside pressure.

TORNADO SAFETY

Tornadoes produce extremely hazardous conditions. The main dangers are caused by extremely high winds and flying debris. Little can be done to prevent heavy damage to structures that are directly hit by a tornado, though good building practices (such as securely fastening the roof of the house to the walls and securing the walls to the foundation) can reduce damage to structures on the periphery of a tornado's circulation. Consequently, most hazard research has been focused on saving lives and reducing injuries.

Surviving a tornado requires an understanding of the hazards and some preparation. The most important step is taking shelter. People are advised not to waste time opening windows to reduce the pressure in a house, since this does no good and flying debris is likely to break the windows before the tornado hits anyway. The best protection in the home can be found under a sturdy table or workbench in the basement. In homes without basements (or when time is extremely limited), the recommendation is to shelter in a small interior room such as a closet or bathroom, preferably one with thick walls and no windows. A mattress can be used as additional cover, and a heavy blanket can protect against dust. It is recommended that people also shield their head and neck with their arms. People are strongly advised to avoid windows in all cases, as flying glass can cause terrible wounds.

Many of the fatalities produced by tornadoes occur in mobile homes. Such homes are very lightly constructed and begin to come apart at relatively low wind speeds. In addition, they can easily be blown over and disintegrate, producing ample amounts of sharp-edged flying debris. Consequently, mobile homes—even ones with anchors or tie-downs—offer no shelter from even very weak tornadoes. At the first indication of possible tornadic activity, residents of mobile homes are advised to seek shelter in sturdy buildings. If no such building is available, it is better to shelter in a ditch or culvert than to remain in the home.

If caught in the open in tornadic conditions, it is recommended to stay low to the ground (preferably in a ditch or culvert) and to hold onto a sturdy object such as a tree stump. The main danger is from being tumbled along the ground by high winds, which can in effect beat a person to death.

It is advised that cars be abandoned as a tornado approaches and that shelter be sought in a ditch. Many tornado-related deaths have occurred in traffic jams, such as those associated with the April 10, 1979, tornado in Wichita Falls, Texas. Cars tend to be tumbled over and over by tornadoes and, in extreme cases, carried aloft and dropped from significant heights. Victims are often thrown from the tumbling car or blown out through the windows.

DEVASTATING TORNADOES

Tornadoes are typically short-duration phenomena. However, occassionally longer-duration events occur. Sometimes thunderstorms can spawn multiple tornadoes that can wreak havoc over vast areas. A few of the more shocking tornadic events of the last 100 years are examined in detail below.

THE TRI-STATE TORNADO OF 1925

The Tri-State Tornado of 1925, which is also called the Great Tri-State Tornado, was the deadliest in U.S. history. It traveled from southeastern Missouri through southern Illinois and into southwestern Indiana on March 18, 1925. The storm completely destroyed a number of towns and caused 695 deaths.

The tornado materialized about 1 PM local time in Ellington, Mo. It caught the town's residents by surprise, as the weather forecast had been normal. (To prevent panic among the public, tornado forecasting was not practiced at the time, and even the word "tornado" had been banned from U.S. weather forecasts since the late 19th century.) The storm moved quickly to the northeast, speeding through the Missouri towns of Annapolis, Biehle, and Frohna and killing 11 people before crossing the Mississippi River into southern Illinois, where it virtually destroyed the towns of Gorham, De Soto, and Murphysboro, among others. Murphysboro was the hardest-hit area in the tornado's path, with 243 fatalities. After killing more than 600 people in Illinois, the tornado crossed the Wabash River into Indiana, where it demolished the towns of Griffin, Owensville, and Princeton and devastated about 85 farms in between.

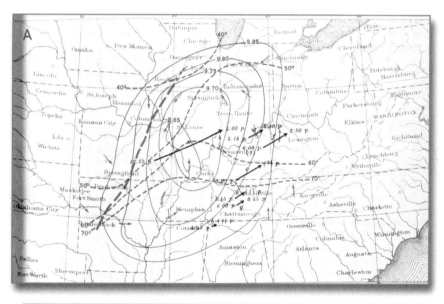

Map outlining the weather conditions and track of the Tri-State Tornado of 1925. The longest-lived tornado on record, the storm killed nearly 700 people across three states. National Oceanic and Atmospheric Administration / Department of Commerce

Having taken 71 lives in Indiana, the storm dissipated about 4:30 PM approximately 5 kilometres (3 miles) southwest of Petersburg.

With winds of roughly 480 kilometres (300 miles) per hour, the tornado lasted 3.5 hours and traveled 352 kilometres (219 miles)—setting records for both duration and distance. Its width of up to 1.6 kilometres (1 mile), average speed of almost 100 kilometres (62 miles) per hour, and peak speed of 117 kilometres (73 miles) per hour also make it one of the largest and fastest tornadoes in U.S. history. In addition to the 695 casualties, there were more than 2,000 injured survivors, as well as thousands who were left homeless and without food. Fires, looting, and theft in the tornado's aftermath exacerbated its effects.

The Palm Sunday Tornado Outbreak of 1965

This outbreak involved a series of tornadoes that struck the Midwestern region of the United States on April 11, 1965. A six-state area of Ohio, Michigan, Indiana, Illinois, Wisconsin, and Iowa was severely damaged by the tornadoes. Indiana's death toll was the heaviest, with 141 of the 270 total deaths. At least 5,000 other persons were injured, and property damage was estimated at more than $250 million.

The Super Outbreak of 1974

The Super Outbreak of 1974 involved a series of tornadoes that caused severe damage to the midwest and east United States and Ontario, Can., on April 3–4, 1974. The largest outbreak of tornadoes ever recorded, it consisted of 144 tornadoes and resulted in more than $1 billion in damage and 330 deaths. The U.S. states affected were Illinois, Indiana, Michigan, Ohio, Kentucky, Tennessee, Alabama, Mississippi, Georgia, North Carolina, Virginia, West Virginia, and New York.

THE SATURIA–MANIKGANJ SADAR TORNADO OF 1989

This catastrophic tornado struck the Manikganj district of Bangladesh on April 26, 1989. Causing approximately 1,300 fatalities, it was likely the deadliest tornado in recorded history.

The tornado struck at around 6:30 PM local time and moved east from the Daulatpur area into the areas of Saturia and Manikganj Sadar—a region that had been suffering from a severe drought. The storm spanned a path that was about 16 kilometres (10 miles) long and about 1.6 kilometres (1 mile) wide. Though confined to a relatively small geographic region (like most other tornadoes) and brief in duration, it completely destroyed all buildings within an area of roughly 6 square kilometres (2.5 square miles). Towns lay in ruins, and tens of thousands of residents were left homeless. In addition, thousands of trees were uprooted and blown away. Though the deadliest, the Saturia–Manikganj Sadar tornado was only one of numerous devastating storms to hit Bangladesh in recent history. On April 17, 1973, another tornado in the Manikganj region had killed at least 681 people.

Chapter 5

TROPICAL STORMS AND TROPICAL CYCLONES

Tropical storms and tropical cyclones develop in ocean basins charaterized by warm water and easterly waves (that is, regions of weak winds centred around areas of low pressure). Both phenomena form and mature the same way. Tropical cyclones are simply more intense. When tropical cyclones strike populated areas, they often cause great amounts of damage, and the strongest ones are capable of tremendous loss of life.

TROPICAL STORMS

Tropical storms are organized centres of low pressure that originate over warm tropical oceans. The maximum sustained surface winds of tropical storms range from 63 to 118 kilometres (39 to 73 miles) per hour. These storms represent an intermediate stage between loosely organized tropical depressions and more intense tropical cyclones. A tropical storm may occur in any of Earth's ocean basins in which tropical cyclones are found (North Atlantic, northeast Pacific, central Pacific, northwest and southwest Pacific, and Indian). The size and structure of tropical storms are similar to those of the more intense and mature tropical cyclones. They possess horizontal dimensions of about 160 kilometres (100 miles) and winds that are highest at the surface but decrease with altitude. The winds typically attain their maximum intensity at approximately 30–50 kilometres (20–30 miles) away from the centre of the circulation, but the distinct eyewall that is a characteristic of mature tropical cyclones is usually absent.

The precursors of tropical storms in the Atlantic are easterly waves that form over Africa and propagate toward the west. The easterly waves are characterized by wind speeds of approximately 16 kilometres (10 miles) per hour and convective clouds that are loosely organized around a central area of low pressure, or trough axis. The winds transfer heat and moisture from the sea surface to the atmosphere. If local atmospheric conditions support deep convection and low vertical wind shear, the system may become organized and begin to intensify. Intensification occurs as the air warmed at the surface begins to rise. The transfer of air away from the centre of the trough axis causes the surface pressure to fall, which in turn causes higher winds that increase the transfer of heat at the surface. The Coriolis force, which is a product of Earth's rotation, causes the winds to rotate about the centre, thereby generating a closed and symmetric circulation pattern.

A similar process occurs in other ocean basins. In the western Pacific, tropical storms originate from loosely organized convection events in the monsoon trough, which is a large-scale area of low pressure that lies along the Equator. The exact mechanism that results in the intensification of the storm is not well understood, but surface pressure falls associated with tropical upper tropospheric troughs (TUTTs) likely play a role.

Once the surface wind speeds in a tropical depression reach 63 kilometres (39 miles) per hour, the regional storm-warning centre assigns a name to the disturbance, and it is classified as a tropical storm. This tropical-storm classification is used until the wind speeds increase above 117 kilometres (73 miles) per hour, in which case the storm is reclassified as a tropical cyclone. In the Atlantic and eastern Pacific, tropical cyclones are classified according to their intensity using the Saffir-Simpson scale (scaled from 1 to 5), a tool used to predict the extent of flooding from rainfall and storm surge and the level of property damage. A "category 1" storm possesses hurricane-force winds in excess of 119 kilometres (74 miles) per hour. Australian forecasters have developed a similar scale, but a category 1 on the Australian scale corresponds to the tropical-storm range of wind speeds.

Since tropical storms are the precursors to the more intense tropical cyclones, they occur more often. The yearly average numbers of tropical storms occurring in the various ocean basins are as follows: North Atlantic has 13, northeastern Pacific has 16, northwestern Pacific has 27, northern Indian has 5, southwestern Indian has 10, and Australian (that is, the southwestern Pacific and southeast Indian basins) has 16. In all ocean basins, roughly 45 percent of the tropical storms continue to intensify to minimal tropical-cyclone strength or greater.

A number of factors may result in the failure of a tropical storm to continue to intensify. In some cases, the storm moves into a region where the large-scale environment does not favour further growth. The sea surface temperature may be too low, the middle atmosphere too dry, or the winds at upper levels too high to support the continued vertical development of the storm. In other cases, the tropical storm makes landfall before reaching hurricane strength and begins to dissipate.

The extreme damage that often accompanies the landfall of tropical cyclones usually does not occur with tropical storms. The lower wind speeds result in a minimal storm surge of less than 4 feet (about 1 metre), and most damage is confined to plants, trees, and unanchored structures, such as mobile homes. Nevertheless, low-lying areas prone to flooding from prolonged periods of rain or mountainous regions subject to flash flooding may be severely impacted by tropical storms. In some regions, rains from tropical systems are an important part of the annual climate and contribute to the total hydrologic cycle.

TROPICAL CYCLONES

Tropical cyclones are stronger versions of tropical storms. They are intense circular storms that originate over warm tropical oceans and are characterized by low atmospheric pressure, high winds, and heavy rain. Drawing energy from the sea surface and maintaining its strength as long as it remains over warm water, a tropical cyclone generates winds that exceed 119 kilometres (74 miles) per hour. In extreme cases winds may exceed 240 kilometres (150 miles) per hour, and gusts may surpass 320 kilometres (200 miles) per hour. Accompanying these strong winds are torrential rains and a devastating phenomenon known as the storm surge, an elevation of the sea surface that can reach 6 metres (20 feet) above normal levels. Such a combination of high winds and water makes cyclones a serious hazard for coastal areas in tropical and subtropical areas of the world. Every year during the late summer months (July–September in the Northern Hemisphere and January–March in the Southern Hemisphere), cyclones strike regions as far apart as the Gulf Coast of North America, northwestern Australia, and eastern India and Bangladesh.

Tropical cyclones are known by various names in different parts of the world. In the North Atlantic Ocean and the eastern North Pacific they are called hurricanes, and in the western North Pacific around the Philippines, Japan, and China the storms are referred to as typhoons.

In the western South Pacific and Indian Ocean they are variously referred to as severe tropical cyclones, tropical cyclones, or simply cyclones. All these different names refer to the same type of storm.

THE ANATOMY OF A CYCLONE

Tropical cyclones are compact, circular storms, generally some 320 kilometres (200 miles) in diameter, whose winds swirl around a central region of low atmospheric pressure. The winds are driven by this low-pressure core and by the rotation of the Earth, which deflects the path of the wind through a phenomenon known as the Coriolis force. As a

Hurricane Humberto rests off the coast of Bermuda in 2001. NASA Goddard Space Flight Center

result, tropical cyclones rotate in a counterclockwise (or cyclonic) direction in the Northern Hemisphere and in a clockwise (or anticyclonic) direction in the Southern Hemisphere.

The wind field of a tropical cyclone may be divided into three regions. First is a ring-shaped outer region, typically having an outer radius of about 160 kilometres (100 miles) and an inner radius of about 30 to 50 kilometres (20 to 30 miles). In this region the winds increase uniformly in speed toward the centre. Wind speeds attain their maximum value at the second region, the eyewall, which is typically 15 to 30 kilometres (10 to 20 miles) from the centre of the storm. The eyewall in turn surrounds the interior region, called the eye, where wind speeds decrease rapidly and the air is often calm. These main structural regions are described in greater detail below.

THE EYE

A characteristic feature of tropical cyclones is the eye, a central region of clear skies, warm temperatures, and low atmospheric pressure. Typically, atmospheric pressure at the surface of the Earth is about 1,000 millibars. At the centre of a tropical cyclone, however, it is typically around 960 millibars, and in a very intense "supertyphoon" of the western Pacific it may be as low as 880 millibars. In addition to low pressure at the centre, there is also a rapid variation of pressure across the storm, with most of the variation occurring near the centre. This rapid variation results in a large pressure gradient force, which is responsible for the strong winds present in the eyewall (described below).

Horizontal winds within the eye, on the other hand, are light. In addition, there is a weak sinking motion, or subsidence, as air is pulled into the eyewall at the surface. As the air subsides, it compresses slightly and warms, so that temperatures at the centre of a tropical cyclone are some 5.5 °C (10 °F) higher than in other regions of the storm. Because warmer air can hold more moisture before condensation occurs, the eye of the cyclone is generally free of clouds. Reports of the air inside the eye being "oppressive" or "sultry" are most likely a psychological response to the rapid change from high winds and rain in the eyewall to calm conditions in the eye.

THE EYEWALL

The most dangerous and destructive part of a tropical cyclone is the eyewall. Here winds are strongest, rainfall is heaviest, and deep convective clouds rise from close to the Earth's surface to a height of 15,000 metres (49,000 feet). As noted above, the high winds are driven by rapid changes in atmospheric pressure near the eye, which creates a large pressure gradient force. Winds actually reach their greatest speed at an altitude of about 300 metres (1,000 feet) above the surface. Closer to the surface they are slowed by friction, and higher than 300 metres (1,000 feet) they are weakened by a slackening of the horizontal pressure gradient force. This slackening is related to the temperature structure of the storm. Air is warmer in the core of a tropical cyclone, and this higher temperature causes atmospheric pressure in the centre to decrease at a slower rate with height than occurs in the surrounding atmosphere. The lessened contrast in atmospheric pressure with altitude causes the horizontal pressure gradient to weaken with height, which in turn results in a decrease in wind speed.

Friction at the surface, in addition to lowering wind speeds, causes the wind to turn inward toward the area of lowest pressure. Air flowing into the low-pressure eye cools by expansion and in turn extracts heat and water vapour from the sea surface. Areas of maximum heating have the strongest updrafts, and the eyewall exhibits the greatest vertical wind speeds in the storm—up to 5 to 10 metres (16.5 to 33 feet) per second, or 18 to 36 kilometres (11 to 22 miles) per hour. While such velocities are much less than those of the horizontal winds, updrafts are vital to the existence of the towering convective clouds embedded in the eyewall. Much of the heavy rainfall associated with tropical cyclones comes from these clouds.

The upward movement of air in the eyewall also causes the eye to be wider aloft than at the surface. As the air spirals upward it conserves its angular momentum, which depends on the distance from the centre of the cyclone and on the wind speed around the centre. Since the wind speed decreases with height, the air must move farther from the centre of the storm as it rises.

When updrafts reach the stable tropopause (the upper boundary of the troposphere, some 16 kilometres [10 miles] above the surface), the air flows outward. The Coriolis force deflects this outward flow, creating a broad anticyclonic circulation aloft. Therefore, horizontal circulation in the upper levels of a tropical cyclone is opposite to that near the surface.

RAINBANDS

In addition to deep convective cells (compact regions of vertical air movement) surrounding the eye, there are often secondary cells arranged in bands around the centre. These bands, commonly called rainbands, spiral into the centre of the storm. In some cases the rainbands are stationary relative to the centre of the moving storm, and in other cases they seem to rotate around the centre. The rotating cloud bands often are associated with an apparent wobbling of the storm track. If this happens as the tropical cyclone approaches a coastline, there may be large differences between the forecast landfall positions and actual landfall.

As a tropical cyclone makes landfall, surface friction increases, which in turn increases the convergence of airflow into the eyewall and the vertical motion of air occurring there. The increased convergence and rising of moisture-laden air is responsible for the torrential rains associated with tropical cyclones, which may be in excess of 250 millimetres (10 inches) in a 24-hour period. At times a storm may stall, allowing heavy rains to persist over an area for several days. In extreme cases, rainfall totals of 760 millimetres (30 inches) in a five-day period have been reported.

THE LIFE OF A CYCLONE

A circulation system goes through a sequence of stages as it intensifies into a mature tropical cyclone. The storm begins as a tropical disturbance, which typically occurs when loosely organized cumulonimbus clouds in an easterly wave begin to show signs of a weak circulation. Once the wind speed increases to 36 kilometres (23 miles) per hour, the storm is classified as a tropical depression. If the circulation continues to intensify and the wind speeds exceed 63 kilometres (39 miles) per hour, then the system is called a tropical storm. Once the maximum wind speed exceeds 119 kilometres (74 miles) per hour, the storm is classified as a tropical cyclone.

There are six conditions favourable for this process to take place. The conditions are listed first below, and then their dynamics are described in greater detail:

- The temperature of the surface layer of ocean water must be 26.5 °C (80 °F) or warmer, and this warm layer must be at least 50 metres (150 feet) deep.

- A preexisting atmospheric circulation must be located near the surface warm layer.
- The atmosphere must cool quickly enough with height to support the formation of deep convective clouds.
- The middle atmosphere must be relatively humid at a height of about 5,000 metres (16,000 feet) above the surface.
- The developing system must be at least 500 kilometres (300 miles) away from the Equator.
- The wind speed must change slowly with height through the troposphere—no more than 10 metres (33 feet) per second between the surface and an altitude of about 10,000 metres (33,000 feet).

TROPICAL CYCLONE FORMATION

The fuel for a tropical cyclone is provided by a transfer of water vapour and heat from the warm ocean to the overlying air, primarily by evaporation from the sea surface. As the warm, moist air rises, it expands and cools, quickly becoming saturated and releasing latent heat through the condensation of water vapour. The column of air in the core of the developing disturbance is warmed and moistened by this process. The temperature difference between the warm, rising air and the cooler environment causes the rising air to become buoyant, further enhancing its upward movement.

If the sea surface is too cool, there will not be enough heat available, and the evaporation rates will be too low to provide the tropical cyclone enough fuel. Energy supplies will also be cut off if the warm surface water layer is not deep enough, because the developing tropical system will modify the underlying ocean. Rain falling from the deep convective clouds will cool the sea surface, and the strong winds in the centre of the storm will create turbulence. If the resulting mixing brings cool water from below the surface layer to the surface, the fuel supply for the tropical system will be removed.

The vertical motion of warm air is by itself inadequate to initiate the formation of a tropical system. However, if the warm, moist air flows into a preexisting atmospheric disturbance, further development will occur. As the rising air warms the core of the disturbance by both release of latent heat and direct heat transfer from the sea surface, the atmospheric pressure in the centre of the disturbance becomes lower. The decreasing pressure causes the surface winds to increase, which in turn increases the vapour and heat transfer and contributes to further rising of air. The warming of the core and the increased surface winds thus reinforce each other in a positive feedback mechanism.

INTENSIFICATION

The dynamics of a tropical cyclone rely on the exterior of a storm being cooler than its core, so it is necessary that the temperature of the atmosphere drop sufficiently rapidly with height. The warm, saturated air rising in the centre of the circulation tends to keep rising as long as the surrounding air is cooler and heavier. This vertical movement allows deep convective clouds to develop. The rising air in the core also draws in some air from the surrounding atmosphere at altitudes of around 5,000 metres (16,000 feet). If this external air is relatively humid, the circulation will continue to intensify. If it is sufficiently dry, then it may evaporate some of the water drops in the rising column, causing the air to become cooler than the surrounding air. This cooling will result in the formation of strong downdrafts that will disrupt the rising motion and inhibit development.

For the development of the rapid rotation characteristic of tropical cyclones, the low-pressure centre must be located at least 500 kilometres (300 miles) away from the Equator. If the initial disturbance is too close to the Equator, then the effect of the Coriolis force will be too small to provide the necessary spin. The Coriolis force deflects the air that is being drawn into the surface low-pressure centre, setting up a cyclonic rotation.

A final requirement for the intensification of tropical cyclones is that there must be little change in the wind speed with height above the surface. If the winds increase too much with altitude, the core of the system will no longer be vertically aligned over the warm surface that provides its energy. The area being warmed and the surface low-pressure centre will move apart, and the positive feedback mechanism described above will be suppressed. Conditions in the tropics that encourage the development of tropical cyclones include a typically minor north-to-south variation in temperature. This relative lack of a temperature gradient causes wind speed to remain relatively constant with height.

DISSIPATION

Tropical cyclones dissipate when they can no longer extract sufficient energy from warm ocean water. As mentioned above, a tropical cyclone can contribute to its own demise by stirring up deeper, cooler ocean waters. In addition, a storm that moves over land will abruptly lose its fuel source and quickly lose intensity.

A tropical cyclone that remains over the ocean and moves into higher latitudes will change its structure and become extratropical as it encounters cooler water. The transformation from a tropical to an extratropical cyclone is marked by an increase in the storm's diameter and by a change in shape from circular to comma- or v-shaped as its rainbands reorganize. An extratropical cyclone typically has a higher central pressure and consequently has lower wind speeds. Extratropical cyclones, which are fueled by a north-to-south variation of temperature, weaken and dissipate in a few days.

TROPICAL CYCLONE DAMAGE

Tropical cyclones are composed of several elements capable of causing death and substantial damage to property. These elements include high winds, the generation of tornadoes upon landfall, gusts and downbursts, storm surge, and heavy rainfall.

HORIZONTAL WINDS

High winds cause some of the most dramatic and damaging effects associated with tropical cyclones. In the most intense tropical cyclones, sustained winds may be as high as 240 kilometres (150 miles) per hour, and gusts can exceed 320 kilometres (200 miles) per hour. The length of time that a given location is exposed to extreme winds depends on the size of the storm and the speed at which it is moving. During a direct hit from a tropical cyclone, an area may endure high winds for several hours. In that time even the most solidly constructed buildings may begin to suffer damage. The force of the wind increases rapidly with its speed. Sustained winds of 100 kilometres (62 miles) per hour exert a pressure of 718 pascals (15 pounds per square foot), while an approximate doubling of wind speed to 200 kilometres (124 miles) per hour increases the pressure almost fivefold to 3,734 pascals. A building with a large surface area facing the wind may be subjected to immense forces. Some of the local variability in damage that is often observed during tropical cyclones is due to the direction that buildings face relative to the prevailing wind.

Horizontal winds associated with a tropical cyclone vary in strength depending on the area of the storm in which they occur. The strongest winds are located in the right-forward quadrant of the storm, as measured along the line that the storm is moving. The intensification of winds in this quadrant is due to the additive effect of winds from the atmospheric flow in which the storm is embedded. For example, in a hurricane approaching the East Coast of the United States, the highest and most damaging winds are located to the northeast of the storm centre.

ASSOCIATION WITH TORNADOES

The intense sustained winds present near the centre of tropical cyclones are responsible for inflicting heavy damage, but there is another wind hazard associated with these storms—tornadoes. Most tropical disturbances that reach storm intensity have tornadoes associated with them when they make landfall, though the tornadoes tend to be weaker than those observed in the Midwestern United States. The number of tornadoes varies, but about 75 percent of tropical cyclones generate fewer than 10. The largest number of tornadoes associated with a tropical cyclone was 141, reported in 1967 as Hurricane Beulah struck the Texas Gulf Coast in the United States.

Tornadoes can occur in any location near the centre of the storm. At distances greater than 50 kilometres (30 miles) from the centre, they are confined to the northeast quadrant of Northern Hemisphere storms and to the southwest quadrant of Southern Hemisphere storms. How the tornadoes are generated is not clear, but surface friction probably plays a role by causing the wind to slow as the tropical cyclone makes landfall. Wind speeds near the surface decrease while those at higher levels are less affected, setting up a low-level horizontal rotation that becomes tilted into the vertical by updrafts, thus providing the concentrated spin required for a tornado.

Gusts, Downbursts, and Swirls

In addition to tornadoes, tropical cyclones generate other localized damaging winds. When a tropical cyclone makes landfall, surface friction decreases wind speed but increases turbulence. This allows fast-moving air aloft to be transported down to the surface, thereby increasing the strength of wind gusts. There is also evidence of tropical cyclone downbursts, driven by evaporative cooling of air. These downbursts are similar to microbursts that may occur during severe thunderstorms. The winds associated with them typically flow in a different direction than those of the cyclone, allowing them to be identified. Other small-scale wind features associated with tropical cyclones are swirls. These are very small, intense, and short-lived vortices that occur under convective towers embedded in the eyewall. They are not classified as tornadoes because their peak winds last only a few seconds. Swirls may rotate in either a counterclockwise or a clockwise direction, and their peak winds are estimated to approach 320 kilometres (200 miles) per hour.

The Storm Surge

In coastal regions an elevation of sea level—the storm surge—is often the deadliest phenomenon associated with tropical cyclones. As previously mentioned, a storm surge accompanying an intense tropical cyclone can be as high as 6 metres (20 feet). Most of the surge is caused by friction between the strong winds in the storm's eyewall and the ocean surface, which piles water up in the direction that the wind is blowing. For tropical cyclones in the Northern Hemisphere this effect is largest in the right-forward quadrant of the storm because the winds are strongest there. In the Southern Hemisphere the left-forward quadrant has the largest storm surge.

A small part of the total storm surge is due to the change in atmospheric pressure across the tropical cyclone. The higher atmospheric pressure at the edges of the storm causes the ocean surface to bulge under the eye, where the pressure is lowest. However, the magnitude of this pressure-induced surge is minimal because the density of water is large compared with that of air. A pressure drop of 100 millibars across the diameter of the storm causes the sea surface under the eye to rise about 1 metre (3 feet).

Flooding caused by the storm surge is responsible for most of the deaths associated with tropical cyclone

Residents fleeing the floods caused by Hurricane Rita in 2005. High winds from hurricanes elevate water levels and push waves toward the shore with great force, creating what is known as a storm surge. © AP Images

landfalls. Extreme examples of storm surge fatalities include 6,000 deaths in Galveston, Texas, in 1900 and the loss of more than 300,000 lives in East Pakistan (now Bangladesh) in 1970 from a storm surge that was estimated to be 9 metres (30 feet) high. Improvements in forecasting the expected height of storm surges and the issuing of warnings are necessary as the population of coastal areas continues to increase.

RAINFALL

Tropical cyclones typically bring large amounts of water into the areas they affect. Much of the water is due to rainfall associated with the deep convective clouds of the eyewall and with the rainbands of the outer edges of the storm. Rainfall rates are typically on the order of several centimetres per hour with shorter bursts of much higher rates. It is not uncommon for totals of 500 to 1,000 millimetres (20 to 40 inches) of rain to be reported over some regions. Rainfall rates such as these may overwhelm the capacity of storm drains, resulting in local flooding. Flooding may be particularly severe in low-lying regions such as in Bangladesh and the Gulf Coast of the United States. It is also a problem in areas where mountains and canyons concentrate the rainfall, as occurred in 1998 when floods caused by rains from Hurricane Mitch washed away entire towns in Honduras.

Another source of high precipitation may be provided by the migration of moist air from the clouds of the mature tropical cyclone. When this moisture moves into areas of low pressure at higher latitudes, significant precipitation may result. An example of this occurred in 1983, when the remnants of the eastern Pacific Hurricane Octave moved into a Pacific cold front that had stalled over the southwestern United States, drenching the Arizona desert with

200 millimetres (8 inches) of rain in a three-day period. On average, that region receives 280 millimetres (11 inches) of rain in an entire year.

THE RANKING AND NAMING OF TROPICAL CYCLONES

Tropical cyclones are ranked by their wind strength at any given point in time. Ranking allows scientists and government officials to prioritize elements of evacuation plans and allocate necessary resources well in advance of the storm's arrival. In addition, since ocean basins are capable of supporting more than one storm at a time, tropical cyclones are issued names to help officials separate one storm from another.

INTENSITY SCALES

A wide range of wind speeds is possible between tropical cyclones of minimal strength and the most intense ones on record, and tropical cyclones can cause damage ranging from the breaking of tree limbs to the destruction of mobile homes and small buildings. To aid in issuing warnings to areas that may be affected by a storm, and to indicate the severity of the potential threat, numerical rating systems have been developed based on a storm's maximum wind speed and potential storm surge.

For tropical systems in the Atlantic and eastern Pacific, the Saffir-Simpson hurricane scale is used. This scale ranks storms that already have reached hurricane strength. A similar scale used to categorize storms near Australia includes both tropical storms and tropical cyclones. Though these two scales have different starting points, the most intense rating in each—category 5—is similar. Numerical ranking scales are not utilized in any of the other ocean basins.

NAMING SYSTEMS

It is not uncommon for more than one tropical cyclonic system to be present in a given ocean basin at any given time. To aid forecasters in identifying the systems and issuing warnings, tropical disturbances are given numbers. When a system intensifies to tropical storm strength, it is given a name.

In the United States, names given to hurricanes during World War II corresponded to radio code names for the letters of the alphabet (such as Able, Baker, and Charlie). In 1953 the U.S. National Weather Service began to identify hurricanes by female names, and in 1978 a series of alternating male and female names came into use. The lists of names are recycled every six years—that is, the 2003 list is used again in 2009, the 2004 list in 2010, and so on.

Names of very intense, damaging, or otherwise newsworthy storms are retired. Names that will not be used again include Gilbert, a 1988 category 5 hurricane that had the lowest central atmospheric pressure (888 millibars) ever recorded in the Atlantic. Also retired is Mitch, the name of a category 5 hurricane that stalled off the coast of Honduras for two days in 1998 before slowly moving inland, inundating Central America with heavy rain and causing mudslides and floods that took nearly 10,000 lives. Another notable storm whose name has been retired was Hurricane Ivan, which reached category 5 on three separate occasions during its long life cycle in September 2004. Ivan almost completely destroyed all agricultural infrastructure in Grenada, wrecked much of that year's crops in Jamaica, leveled 1.1 million hectares (2.7 million acres) of timber in Alabama, and caused almost 100 deaths along its path.

Pacific and Indian basin storms are named according to systems established by regional committees under the auspices of the World Meteorological Organization. Each region maintains its own list of names, and changes to the list (such as retiring a name) are ratified at formal meetings. Two or more lists of names are alternated each year for several regions, including the central North Pacific (i.e., the Hawaii region), the western North Pacific and South China Sea, the southern Indian Ocean west of 90° E, the western South Pacific Ocean, and Australia's eastern, central, and northern ocean regions. In some areas, such as the northern Indian Ocean, tropical cyclones are given numbers instead of names.

THE LOCATION AND PATTERNS OF TROPICAL CYCLONES

The formation and development of tropical cyclones are limited to warm regions of Earth's oceans where warm ocean water interacts with favourable wind systems. Once formed, tropical cyclones tend to drift westward and poleward driven by the trade winds, subsiding air from the subtropical highs, and the Coriolis force.

OCEAN BASINS AND PEAK SEASONS

Tropical oceans spawn approximately 80 tropical storms annually, and about two-thirds are severe (category 1 or higher on the Saffir-Simpson scale of intensity). Almost 90 percent of these storms form within 20° north or south of the Equator. Poleward of those latitudes, sea surface temperatures are too cool to allow tropical cyclones to form, and mature storms moving that far north or south will begin to dissipate. Only two tropical ocean basins do not support tropical cyclones, because they lack waters that are sufficiently warm. The Peru Current in the eastern South Pacific and the Benguela Current in the South Atlantic carry cool water Equatorward from higher latitudes and so deter tropical cyclone development. The Pacific Ocean generates the greatest number of tropical storms and cyclones. The most powerful storms, sometimes called supertyphoons, occur in the western Pacific. The Indian Ocean is second in the total number of storms, and the Atlantic Ocean ranks third.

Tropical cyclones are warm season phenomena. The peak frequency of these storms occurs after the maximum in solar radiation is received for the year, which occurs on June 22 in the Northern Hemisphere and December 22 in the Southern Hemisphere. The ocean surface reaches its maximum temperature several weeks after the solar radiation maximum, so most tropical cyclones occur during the late summer to early fall—that is, from July to September in the Northern Hemisphere and from January to March in the Southern Hemisphere.

FAVOURABLE WIND SYSTEMS

The lower latitudes are favourable for the generation of tropical cyclones not only because of their warm ocean waters but also because of the general atmospheric circulation of the region. Tropical cyclones originate from loosely organized, large-scale circulation systems such as those associated with the strong, low-level easterly jet over Africa. This jet generates easterly waves—regions of low atmospheric pressure that have a maximum intensity at an altitude of about 3,600 metres (12,000 feet) and a horizontal extent of about 2,400 kilometres (1,500 miles). Most of the tropical cyclones in the Atlantic and eastern North Pacific begin as easterly waves. Given favourable conditions, an easterly wave may intensify and contract horizontally, ultimately resulting in the characteristic circulation of a tropical cyclone. In the western Pacific, large areas of upper-level low pressure help pull air from the centre of the developing disturbances and thus contribute to a drop in surface atmospheric pressure. It is these features, known as tropical upper tropospheric troughs, or TUTTs, that are responsible for the large number of tropical cyclones in the western Pacific.

In some cases, external geographic factors aid in development of tropical cyclones. The mountains of Mexico and Central America modify easterly waves that move through the Caribbean and into the eastern Pacific. This often results in closed circulations at low levels over the eastern Pacific Ocean, many of which develop into tropical cyclones.

TROPICAL CYCLONE TRACKS

Tropical cyclones in both the Northern and Southern Hemispheres tend to move westward and drift slowly poleward. Their motion is due in large part to the general circulation of the Earth's atmosphere. Surface winds in the tropics, known as the trade winds, blow from east to west, and they are responsible for the general westward motion of tropical cyclones. For the poleward movement, two other factors are responsible. One is the presence of large-scale regions of subsiding air, known as subtropical highs, over the oceans poleward of the trade winds. These regions of high atmospheric pressure have anticyclonic circulations (that is, clockwise circulation in the Northern Hemisphere and counterclockwise in the Southern), so that winds on the western edges of these large-scale circulations move toward the poles. The second factor is the Coriolis force, which becomes progressively stronger at higher latitudes. The diameter of a tropical cyclone is large enough for the Coriolis force to influence its poleward side more strongly, and hence the tropical cyclone is deflected toward the pole. Once a tropical cyclone moves poleward of the subtropical high, it begins to move eastward under the influence of the middle-latitude westerlies

205

(which blow toward the east). When the motion of a tropical cyclone changes from westward to eastward, the tropical cyclone is said to recurve.

Tropical cyclones in the Northern Hemisphere can travel to higher latitudes than in the Southern Hemisphere because of the presence of warm clockwise oceanic currents such as the Kuroshio and the Gulf Stream. In the North Atlantic the warm waters of the Gulf Stream supply energy to hurricanes as they move along the east coast of the United States, allowing them to survive for a longer time. It is not uncommon for very intense tropical systems to make landfall as far north as Boston (42° N). On the other hand, hurricanes do not make landfall on the west coast of the United States even though prevailing winds over the North Pacific Ocean move eastward toward land. Instead, they tend to weaken rapidly as they recurve because they are moving over cooler ocean waters.

TRACKING AND FORECASTING

In the first half of the 20th century the identification of tropical cyclones was based on changes in weather conditions, the state of the sea surface, and reports from areas that had already been affected by the storm. This method left little time for advance warning and contributed to high death tolls. Observation networks and techniques improved with time. With the advent of weather satellites in the 1960s, the early detection and tracking of tropical cyclones was greatly improved.

THE USE OF SATELLITES AND AIRCRAFT

An array of geostationary satellites (those that remain over a fixed position on the Earth) is operated by a number of countries. Each of these satellites provides continuous displays of the Earth's surface in visible light and in infrared

"Supertyphoon" Chaba (right) *approaching Japan and Typhoon Aere* (left) *hitting Taiwan, as photographed by the GOES-9 satellite, Aug. 25, 2004.* NOAA

wavelengths. It is the latter that are most important in tracking the stages of tropical cyclone development. Infrared images show the temperatures of cloud tops, thus allowing the loosely organized convection associated with easterly waves to be detected by the presence of cold, high clouds. They also show the deep, organized convection characteristic of a tropical cyclone. Satellite images not only show a storm's location but also can be used to estimate its intensity because certain cloud patterns are characteristic of particular wind speeds.

Although satellite images provide general information on the location and intensity of tropical cyclones, detailed information on a storm's strength and structure must be obtained directly, using aircraft. This information is essential in providing the most accurate warnings possible. Operational reconnaissance is done only by the United

States for storms that may affect its continental landmass. No other country does this type of reconnaissance. Tropical cyclones in other ocean basins occur over a larger region, and most countries do not have the financial resources to maintain research aircraft. When evidence of a developing circulation is detected in the Atlantic or Caribbean, a U.S. Air Force C-130 aircraft is dispatched to determine if a closed circulation is present. The centre of circulation is noted, and an instrument called a dropsonde is released through the bottom of the aircraft to measure the temperature, humidity, atmospheric pressure, and wind speed. In many cases, the naming of a tropical storm, or its upgrade from tropical storm to tropical cyclone, is based on aircraft observations.

LANDFALL FORECASTS

Tropical storms developing in the world's ocean basins are tracked by various national weather services that have been designated Regional Specialized Meteorological Centres (RSMCs) by the World Meteorological Organization (WMO). The RSMCs are located at Miami, Florida, and Honolulu, Hawaii, U.S.; Tokyo, Japan; Nadi, Fiji; Darwin, Northern Territory, Australia; New Delhi, India; and Saint-Denis, Réunion. Warnings are also issued for more limited regions by Tropical Cyclone Warning Centres in a number of locations, including Port Moresby, Papua New Guinea; Wellington, New Zealand; and Perth, Western Australia, and Brisbane, Queensland, Australia. In addition, the Joint Typhoon Warning Centers in Hawaii are responsible for U.S. military forecasts in the western Pacific and Indian Oceans, which overlap a number of WMO regions of responsibility.

Forecasting hurricane landfall and providing warnings for storms that will effect the United States is done by the National Hurricane Center in Miami. Forecasters use a variety of observational information from satellites and aircraft to determine the current location and intensity of the storm. This information is used along with computer forecast models to predict the future path and intensity of the storm. There are three basic types of computer models. The simplest ones use statistical relations based on the typical paths of hurricanes in a region, along with the assumption that the current observed motion of the storm will persist. A second type of model, called a statistical-dynamical model, forecasts the large-scale circulation by solving equations that describe changes in atmospheric pressure, wind, and moisture. Statistical relations that predict the track of the storm based on the large-scale conditions are then used to forecast the storm's future position. A third type of model is a purely dynamic forecast model. In this model, equations are solved that describe changes in both the large-scale circulation and the tropical cyclone itself. Dynamic forecast models show the interaction of the tropical cyclone with its environment, but they require the use of large and powerful computers as well as very complete descriptions of the structure of the tropical cyclone and that of the surrounding environment. Computer models currently do well in forecasting the path of tropical cyclones, but they are not as reliable in forecasting changes in intensity more than 24 hours in advance.

Once forecasters have determined that a tropical cyclone is likely to make landfall, warnings are issued for the areas that may be affected. The forecasters provide a "best-track" forecast, which is an estimate of the track and maximum wind speed over a period of 72 hours based on all available observations and computer model results. Strike probability forecasts are issued that indicate probabilities (in percentages) that the tropical cyclone will affect a given area over a given time interval. These forecasts allow local authorities to begin warning and evacuation plans. As the storm approaches, a tropical cyclone watch is issued for areas that may be threatened. In especially vulnerable areas, evacuation may be initiated based on the watch. If tropical cyclone conditions are expected in an area within 24 hours, a tropical cyclone warning is issued. Once a warning is issued, evacuation is recommended for areas prone to storm surges and areas that may be isolated by high water.

LONG-TERM FORECASTS

Forecasts of expected numbers of Atlantic tropical cyclones are now being made well in advance of the start of each year's tropical cyclone season. The forecast model takes into account seasonal trends in factors related to tropical cyclone formation such as the presence of El Niño or La Niña oceanic conditions, amount of rainfall over Africa, winds in the lower stratosphere, and atmospheric pressure and wind tendencies over the Caribbean. Based on these factors, forecasts are issued concerning the expected numbers of tropical storms, tropical cyclones, and intense tropical cyclones for the Atlantic. These forecasts are issued in December, and they are revised in June and again in August of each year for the current Atlantic tropical cyclone season. The forecast model has displayed reasonable skill in predicting the total number of storms each season.

CLIMATIC VARIATIONS AND
TROPICAL CYCLONE FREQUENCY

The number of tropical cyclones generated during a given a year has been observed to vary with certain climatic conditions that modify the general circulation of the atmosphere. One of these conditions is the intermittent occurrence of El Niño, an oceanic phenomenon characterized by the presence every few years of unusually warm water over the equatorial eastern Pacific. The presence of unusually cool surface waters in the region is known as La Niña. While the factors connecting El Niño and La Niña to tropical cyclones are complicated, there are a few general relationships. During years when El Niño conditions are present, upper-level winds over the Atlantic tend to be stronger than normal, which increases the vertical shear and decreases tropical cyclone activity. La Niña conditions result in weaker shear and enhanced tropical cyclone activity. The variation of sea surface temperature associated with El Niño and La Niña also changes the strength and location of the jet stream, which in turn alters the tracks of tropical cyclones. There are indications that El Niño and La Niña modulate tropical cyclone activity in other parts of the world as well. More tropical cyclones seem to occur in the eastern portion of the South Pacific during El Niño years, and fewer occur during La Niña years.

The possibility is being examined that changes in the Earth's climate might alter the numbers, intensity, or paths of tropical cyclones worldwide. Increasing the amount of carbon dioxide and other greenhouse gases in the atmosphere through the burning of fossil fuels and other human activities may increase the global average temperature—and the temperature of the sea surface. These potential changes would influence the maximum intensity reached by a tropical cyclone, which depends on both the sea surface temperature and the temperature of the upper troposphere. An increase in global temperature, however, could actually decrease the number of tropical cyclones because any change in temperature would be accompanied by changes in the Earth's general circulation. If tropical atmospheric circulation were to change in such a way as to increase the winds at upper levels, then there could be a decrease in tropical cyclone activity. An assessment by the World Meteorological Organization of the effect of climate change on tropical cyclones concluded that there is no evidence to suggest that an enhanced greenhouse effect will cause any major changes in the global location of tropical cyclone genesis or the total area of the Earth's surface over which tropical cyclones form. Furthermore, while the maximum potential intensity of tropical cyclones may increase by 10 to 20 percent with a doubling of the concentration of carbon dioxide in the atmosphere, factors such as increased cooling due to ocean spray and changes in the vertical temperature variation may offset these effects.

SIGNIFICANT CYCLONES

Although several tropical cyclones occur each year, a few have been particularly notable for their size, measured wind speeds, the number of deaths, or amount of property damage they cause.

THE KAMIKAZE OF 1274 AND 1281

A pair of massive typhoons each wrecked a Mongol fleet attempting to invade Japan in 1274 and 1281. The storms destroyed most of the Mongol ships and dispersed the rest, forcing the attackers to abandon their plans and fortuitously saving Japan from foreign conquest.

The two Mongol fleets were dispatched by Kublai Khan, the grandson of Genghis Khan who had conquered China and had become the first emperor of its Yuan (Mongol) dynasty. The first invasion force that attacked Japan in the autumn of 1274 comprised about 30,000 to 40,000 men (mostly ethnic Chinese and Koreans, except for the Mongolian officers) and an estimated 500 to 900 vessels. The typhoon struck as the ships lay at anchor in

Hakata Bay, Kyushu, Japan, sinking about one-third of them, with the rest limping home. It is estimated that 13,000 of Kublai's men drowned.

The second Mongol fleet was much larger, made up of two separate forces—one setting out from Masan (Korea) and the other sailing from southern China—with a combined force of 4,400 vessels and some 140,000 soldiers and sailors. The two fleets joined up near Hakata Bay, again the main point of attack, on Aug. 12, 1281. On August. 15, as they were about to assault the much smaller Japanese forces defending the island (about 40,000 samurai and other fighting men), a massive typhoon hit, wrecking the Mongol fleet and once again foiling the invasion attempt. The invading forces suffered tremendous casualties, with at least half the Mongol warriors drowning and all but a few hundred ships from the fleet perishing during the storm. Most of the men who survived the storm were hunted down and killed by the samurai over the following days. Only a small fraction of Kublai Khan's original force returned home from this ill-fated expedition, one of the largest and most disastrous attempts at a naval invasion in history.

Literally meaning "divine wind," the term *kamikaze* was coined in honour of the 1281 typhoon, as it was perceived to be a gift from the gods, supposedly granted after a retired emperor went on a pilgrimage and prayed for divine intervention. The term was later used in World War II to refer to the Japanese suicide pilots who deliberately crashed their planes into enemy targets, usually ships.

THE GREAT HURRICANE OF 1780

This event occurred in the Caribbean Sea in October 1780. It was one of the deadliest on record in the Atlantic Ocean. More than 20,000 people were killed as the storm swept through the eastern Caribbean Sea, with the greatest loss of life centred on the Antilles islands of Barbados, Martinique, and Sint Eustatius.

The hurricane took place before modern tracking of tropical storms began, but historical accounts indicate that the storm started in the Atlantic and on Oct. 10 reached Barbados, where it destroyed nearly all the homes on the island and left few trees standing. Witness reports in Barbados and Saint Lucia claimed that even sturdy stone buildings and forts were completely lost to the wind, with heavy cannons being carried hundreds of feet. The storm traveled northwest across the Antilles, causing destruction throughout the region; on some islands entire towns disappeared. The storm ravaged Martinique, taking an estimated 9,000 lives. On the island of Sint Eustatius an estimated 4,000 to 5,000 people were killed. During this time, European naval forces were concentrated in the Caribbean because of the American Revolution, and both British and French forces sustained particularly large losses, with more than 40 French vessels sunk near Martinique and roughly 4,000 soldiers dead. As the storm continued north, it damaged or sank many other ships that were returning to Europe.

THE BENGAL CYCLONE OF 1876

This deadly cyclone, which is also called the Great Backerganj cyclone of 1876, struck Bangladesh (then part of the province of Bengal in British India) on Oct. 31, 1876, killing approximately 200,000 people.

The cyclone formed over the Bay of Bengal and made landfall at the Meghna River estuary. A high tide made the effects of the storm particularly deadly, and a storm surge of roughly 40 feet (12 metres) flooded the low-lying coastal areas. It is estimated that half of the deaths caused by the storm resulted from disease and starvation related to the flooding.

THE HAIPHONG CYCLONE OF 1881

Striking Southeast Asia on Oct. 8, 1881, the Haiphong cyclone was one of most catastrophic natural disasters in history and the third deadliest tropical cyclone ever recorded. The cyclone smashed into the Gulf of Tonkin, setting off tidal waves that flooded the city of Haiphong in northeastern Vietnam, caused widespread destruction, and killed an estimated 300,000 inhabitants.

Located on a branch of the Red River delta on its northeastern edge, the port city of Haiphong is situated about 16 km (10 miles) inland from the Gulf of Tonkin. It is connected to the sea by an access channel, which, during the storm, magnified the extent of the flooding and destruction. Developed as a seaport by the French starting in 1874, the city had always been crucial to the economy of the region (today, it functions as the outport of the capital, Hanoi). Thus, the effects of the cyclone were devastating to the region. The storm's direct death toll of 300,000 (more are thought to have died of disease and starvation later) ranks it behind only the Ganges-Brahmaputra delta ("Bhola") cyclone that devastated East Pakistan (now Bangladesh) in 1970 and the Hugli (Hooghly) River cyclone that hit the Bengal region of the Indian subcontinent in 1737. The exact category and strength of the Haiphong cyclone are not known, as is the case for many meteorological events and natural disasters that took place before the 20th century.

THE GALVESTON HURRICANE OF 1900

This event, which is also known as the Great Galveston hurricane, occurred in September 1900. It was one of the deadliest natural disasters in U.S. history, claiming more than 5,000 lives. As the storm hit the island city of Galveston, Texas, it was a category 4 hurricane, the second-strongest designation on the Saffir-Simpson hurricane scale.

The storm was first detected on Aug. 27 in the tropical Atlantic. The system landed on Cuba as a tropical storm on Sept. 3 and moved on in a west-northwest direction. In the Gulf of Mexico the storm rapidly intensified. Citizens along the Gulf Coast were warned that the hurricane was approaching. However, many ignored the warnings. On Sept. 8 the storm reached Galveston, which at the time had a population of approximately 40,000 and benefited economically and culturally from its status as the largest port city in Texas. The storm tides of 2.5–4.5 metres (8–15 feet) and winds at more than 210 kilometres (130 miles) per hour were too much for the low-lying city. Homes and businesses were easily demolished by the water and wind, and thousands of lives were lost. From Galveston, the storm moved on to the Great Lakes and New England, which experienced strong wind gusts and heavy rainfall.

After the hurricane, Galveston raised the elevation of many new buildings by more than 3 metres (10 feet). The city also built an extensive seawall to act as a buffer against future storms. Despite the reconstruction, the city's status as the premier shipping port was lost to Houston a few years after the disaster.

THE ISE BAY TYPHOON OF 1959

Also known as Super Typhoon Vera, the Ise Bay typhoon was the most destructive tropical cyclones in Japanese history. The storm struck the Ise Bay region on the southern coast of Japan's main island, Honshu, on Sept. 26, 1959, and wreaked havoc in the city of Nagoya. The storm killed more than 5,000 people, left an estimated 1.5 million people homeless, and injured almost 39,000 people.

The storm began as a low-pressure area in the Pacific Ocean on Sept. 20, gaining strength as it moved north-westward. On Sept. 21 the storm was classified as a typhoon, and it continued to intensify as it moved toward Japan. When the storm made landfall in the Ise Bay region of Japan on Sept. 26, its winds were as high as 260 kilometres (160 miles) per hour—the equivalent of a category 5 storm on the Saffir-Simpson hurricane scale. Because of the strength of the storm, its effects were devastating. Coastal sea walls were destroyed, and strong storm surges caused widespread flooding in the region. Thousands of buildings were completely destroyed, and in some areas drinking water was contaminated. Because of extensive rainfall, rivers flooded and crops were ruined. Thousands of people were stranded as some areas became completely inaccessible. This, combined with a lack of shelter, contributed to the high death count. Under these inhospitable conditions, dysentery became prevalent, along with gangrene and tetanus.

The extensive damage caused by the typhoon was a huge blow to Japan's economy, which was still recovering from World War II. As a result of the storm, the Japanese government created a disaster management council to ensure that national and regional governments would have measures in place to provide more effective emergency assistance in the aftermath of future storms.

HURRICANE CAMILLE 1969

This tropical cyclone, which made landfall in the southern United States in August 1969, was one of the strongest of the 20th century. After entering the Gulf of Mexico, the hurricane struck the Mississippi River basin. As the storm moved inland across much of the southeastern United States and Appalachia, it caused severe flash flooding.

Hurricane Camille started as a tropical storm on Aug. 14, 1969, west of the Cayman Islands and rapidly gained strength as it moved toward Cuba. On Aug. 16 the storm was a category 5 hurricane, the highest classification on the Saffir-Simpson hurricane scale. Late on the night of Aug. 17, the storm hit Bay Saint Louis in Mississippi. Camille's gusts were powerful enough to knock out all wind-recording instruments, leaving some experts estimating wind speed at more than 320 kilometres (200 miles) per hour. Parts of the Gulf of Mexico coast experienced tides more than 7 metres (24 feet) high. As the storm moved northeast through the Ohio Valley and into Virginia, it weakened to a tropical depression. Before it entered the Atlantic Ocean on Aug. 20, Camille dumped 300–500 millimetres (12–20 inches) of rain in parts of West Virginia and Virginia, which experienced devastating floods and landslides.

Wreckage along the Mississippi Gulf Coast in the aftermath of Hurricane Camille, one of the strongest tropical cyclones of the 20th century. National Oceanic and Atmospheric Administration/Department of Commerce

Before the hurricane made landfall, projections of the path of the storm varied. More than 150,000 people were instructed to evacuate their homes. Most left the affected areas in time, but ultimately, more than 250 people were killed. In addition to the loss of life, there were major economic losses resulting from storm damage as well as the relief and recovery efforts that followed.

THE GANGES-BRAHMAPUTRA DELTA CYCLONE OF 1970

The Ganges-Brahmaputra delta cyclone, or Bhola cyclone, was a catastrophic tropical cyclone that struck East Pakistan (now Bangladesh) on Nov. 12, 1970, killing hundreds of thousands of people in the densely populated Ganges-Brahmaputra delta. Even though it was not ranked in the top category of cyclone intensity scales, it was perhaps the deadliest tropical cyclone in recorded history and one of the greatest natural disasters.

The cyclone formed over the Bay of Bengal on Nov. 8, 1970. After reaching its peak wind speed of 185 kilometres (115 miles) per hour, it made landfall on the coast of East Pakistan on Nov. 12. The cyclone was accompanied by a storm surge (a rapid elevation of sea level) that flooded the low-lying region. An estimated 300,000 to 500,000 residents were killed, mostly through drowning, and entire villages were wiped out.

The Pakistani government's handling of the rescue and relief operations was severely criticized by both the international media and local political leaders in East Pakistan. Mounting frustration with relief efforts contributed to a victory for opposition politicians in the national elections held a month after the cyclone. The deteriorating political conditions culminated in a war that ended in 1971 with East Pakistan's independence as the new country of Bangladesh.

THE BANGLADESH CYCLONE OF 1991

Occurring from April 22 to April 30, 1991, this event was one of the deadliest tropical cyclones ever recorded. The storm hit near the Chittagong region, one of the most populated areas in Bangladesh. An estimated 140,000 people were killed by the storm, as many as 10 million people lost their homes, and overall property damage was in the billions of dollars.

The weather system originated in the Bay of Bengal and began moving north. By April 24 the storm was designated Tropical Storm 02B, and by April 28 it was a tropical cyclone. One day later the storm hit south of Chittagong, with winds of up to 240 kilometres (150 miles) per hour. The damage was immediate, as a storm surge as high as 5 metres (15 feet) engulfed the flat, coastal plans of southeastern Bangladesh. The surge washed away entire villages and swamped farms, destroying crops and spreading fears of widespread hunger as well as economic woes. Worries were exacerbated by the memory of the Ganges-Brahmaputra delta ("Bhola") cyclone of 1970, which had taken the lives of as many as 500,000 people in what was then East Pakistan (now Bangladesh). As a result of the 1970 storm, a few storm shelters had been built. Though in 1991 some were saved by the shelters, many people had doubted warnings of the storm or had been given inadequate warning.

Since the 1991 storm, the Bangladesh government has built thousands of elevated shelters in coastal areas believed to be most vulnerable to cyclones. In addition the government has started a reforestation program designed to alleviate future flooding.

HURRICANE ANDREW 1992

Hurricane Andrew ravaged the The Bahamas, southern Florida, and south-central Louisiana in late August 1992.

220

At the time, it was the most expensive Atlantic hurricane in U.S. history (later surpassed by Hurricane Katrina in 2005).

Hurricane Andrew began as a tropical depression off the west coast of Africa near the Cape Verde Islands on Aug. 16. The next day it was classified as a tropical storm by the National Hurricane Center of the U.S. National Weather Service. After traveling west-northwest across the Atlantic Ocean, it turned northwest, avoiding the islands of the eastern Caribbean Sea. On Aug. 20, the strength of the storm declined considerably. (A measurement taken near the centre of the storm revealed that Andrew's atmospheric pressure was 1,015 millibars at this time. Tropical storms and hurricanes typically possess atmospheric pressures lower than 1,000 millibars.) By Aug. 21, fueled by the presence of a nearby low-pressure cell, Andrew reintensified. It became a hurricane on Aug. 22, developing into a category 5 storm on the Saffir-Simpson hurricane scale the following day. It made landfall on Eleuthera, The Bahamas, on Aug. 23 with winds of 259 kilometres (161 miles) per hour.

After weakening slightly over The Bahamas, Andrew strengthened once again over the Straits of Florida before reaching the southern tip of Florida on the morning of Aug. 24. Shortly before landfall, an instrument called a dropsonde that had been released from an aircraft into the centre of the storm recorded an atmospheric pressure of 932 millibars. When Hurricane Andrew struck the coast of Florida, the storm's wind speed was 268 kilometres (166.8 miles) per hour, with at least one gust reaching 285 kilometres (177 miles) per hour. Andrew quickly traveled due west across the peninsula and diminished to a category 3 hurricane. When it made landfall in southern Louisiana on Aug. 26, the winds had dropped to 185 kilometres (115 miles) per hour.

Storm-related damage to The Bahamas was estimated at $250 million, whereas damage to property in the United States was roughly $26.5 billion. The hardest hit area was Dade county in southeastern Florida, where the storm destroyed over 25,000 homes and damaged an additional 100,000. The hurricane caused 26 direct and 39 indirect deaths, the majority occurring in Dade county. In 1993 the name Andrew was retired for hurricanes by the World Meteorological Organization.

HURRICANE MITCH 1998

Hurricane Mitch devastated Central America, particularly Honduras and Nicaragua, in late October 1998. Hurricane Mitch was recognized as the second deadliest Atlantic hurricane on record, after the Great Hurricane of 1780. With millions left homeless and property damage of roughly $6 billion, it was also one of the most destructive.

Hurricane Mitch formed as a tropical depression in the southwestern Caribbean Sea on Oct. 22. After being upgraded to a hurricane on Oct. 24, Mitch entered a period of rapid intensification, and, by the afternoon of Oct. 26, it had grown into a category 5 hurricane. It reached its peak wind speed of 290 kilometres (180 miles) per hour off the northeastern coast of Honduras on Oct. 26 and 27, when it dumped heavy rain on much of Central America, particularly on Honduras and Nicaragua. As the storm weakened and stalled near the northern coast of Honduras, the rains increased in intensity, causing flash floods and mud slides, which devastated coastal regions and the Honduran island of Guanaja.

Mitch made landfall in northern Honduras on Oct. 29 and then moved slowly inland while continuing to produce tremendous amounts of rain. The rains reached a rate of about 100 millimetres (4 inches) per hour, with total rainfall exceeding 750 millimetres (30 inches) along the coast and 1,250 millimetres (50 inches) in the interior areas. After wreaking havoc on Central America, Hurricane Mitch moved east-northeast, regaining its strength in the Bay of Campeche and hitting Florida as a tropical storm on Nov. 5. After clearing Florida, it finally dissipated over the Atlantic.

The floods, mud slides, and wind damaged Honduras's entire infrastructure, ruined its agricultural crops, and demolished population centres throughout the country. Parts of Nicaragua, Guatemala, Belize, and El Salvador were also devastated, with hundreds of thousands of homes obliterated, residents swept away, and crops wiped out. The storm killed more than 11,000 people (mostly in Honduras and Nicaragua, but also in Guatemala, El Salvador, Mexico, and Costa Rica), and thousands more were missing afterward.

Reconstruction projects were extensive and time-consuming, particularly in Honduras and Nicaragua. International relief efforts provided significant help. In 1999 the name Mitch was retired for hurricanes by the World Meteorological Organization.

HURRICANE KATRINA 2005

Striking the southeastern United States in late August 2005, Hurricane Katrina and its aftermath claimed more than 1,800 lives. It is ranked as the costliest natural disaster in U.S. history.

The storm that would later become Hurricane Katrina surfaced on Aug. 23, 2005, as a tropical depression over the Bahamas, approximately 560 kilometres (350 miles) east of Miami. Over the next two days the weather system gathered strength, earning the designation Tropical Storm Katrina, and it made landfall between Miami and Fort Lauderdale, Fla., as a category 1 hurricane (a storm that,

Satellite image of Hurricane Katrina as it approached landfall along the gulf coast of the United States, Aug. 27, 2005. On that date, the Katrina had been classified as a Category 3 hurricane. NASA/SVS

on the Saffir-Simpson scale, exhibits winds in the range of 119–154 kilometres [74–95 miles] per hour). Sustained winds of 115 kilometres (70 miles) per hour lashed the Florida peninsula, and rainfall totals of 13 centimetres (5 inches) were reported in some areas. The storm spent less than eight hours over land. It quickly intensified when it reached the warm waters of the Gulf of Mexico.

On Aug. 27 Katrina strengthened to a category 3 hurricane, with top winds exceeding 185 kilometres (115 miles) per hour and a circulation that covered virtually the entire Gulf of Mexico. By the following afternoon Katrina had become one of the most powerful Atlantic storms on record, with winds in excess of 275 kilometres (170 miles) per hour. On the morning of Aug. 29, the storm made landfall as a category 4 hurricane at Plaquemines Parish,

La., approximately 70 kilometres (45 miles) southeast of New Orleans. It continued on a course to the northeast, crossing the Mississippi Sound and making a second land-fall later that morning near the mouth of the Pearl River. A storm surge more than 8 metres (26 feet) high slammed into the coastal cities of Gulfport and Biloxi, Miss., devastating homes and resorts along the beachfront.

In New Orleans, where much of the greater metropolitan area is below sea level, federal officials initially believed that the city had "dodged the bullet." While New Orleans had been spared a direct hit by the intense winds of the storm, the true threat was soon apparent. The levee system that held back the waters of Lake Pontchartrain and Lake Borgne had been completely overwhelmed by 25

Satellite image of Hurricane Katrina taken on Aug. 28, 2005. By then, Katrina's wind strength had increased, and had became one of the most powerful Atlantic storms on record. NOAA

centimetres (10 inches) of rain and Katrina's storm surge. Areas east of the Industrial Canal were the first to flood. By the afternoon of Aug. 29, some 20 percent of the city was underwater.

New Orleans Mayor Ray Nagin had ordered a mandatory evacuation of the city the previous day, and an estimated 1.2 million people left ahead of the storm. However, tens of thousands of residents could not or would not leave. They either remained in their homes or sought shelter at locations such as the New Orleans Convention Center or the Louisiana Superdome. As the already strained levee system continued to give way, the remaining residents of New Orleans were faced with a city that by Aug. 30 was 80 percent underwater. Many local agencies found themselves unable to respond to the increasingly desperate situation, as their own headquarters and control centres were under 6 metres (20 feet) of water. With no relief in sight, and in the absence of an organized effort to restore order, looting became widespread.

On Aug. 31 the first wave of evacuees arrived at the Red Cross shelter at the Houston Astrodome, some 560 kilometres (350 miles) away from New Orleans, but tens of thousands remained in the city. By Sept. 1 an estimated 30,000 people were seeking shelter under the damaged roof of the Superdome, and an additional 25,000 had gathered at the Convention Center. Shortages of food and potable water quickly became an issue, and daily temperatures reached 32 °C (90 °F). An absence of basic sanitation combined with the omnipresent bacteria-rich floodwaters to create a public health emergency.

It was not until Sept. 2 that an effective military presence was established in the city and National Guard troops mobilized to distribute food and water. The

New Orleans residents displaced by Hurricane Katrina await evacuation outside the Superdrome. Tens of thousands sought safety at the arena as Katrina bore down on the city. Mario Tama/Getty Images

evacuation of hurricane victims continued, and crews began to rebuild the breached levees. On Sept. 6, local police estimated that there were fewer than 10,000 residents left in New Orleans. As the recovery began, dozens of countries contributed funds and supplies, and Canada and Mexico deployed troops to the Gulf Coast to assist with the cleanup and rebuilding. U.S. Army engineers pumped the last of the floodwaters out of the city on Oct. 11, 2005, some 43 days after Katrina made landfall. Ultimately, the storm caused more than $80 billion in damage, and it reduced the population of New Orleans to a fraction of its former size. In 2005 the name Katrina was retired for hurricanes by the World Meteorological Organization.

THE ROLE OF EARTH'S
VIOLENT WINDS

Tornadoes, tropical cyclones, and other violent winds are among the most spectacular natural events. These weather events rival floods, earthquakes, and large volcanoes in the number of deaths and the amount of damage they cause. However, they also occur with alarming regularity over a wider area. Much of the world's tropical and subtropical coasts are vulnerable to tropical cyclones, whereas tornadoes and other violent winds occur seasonally in the middle and high latitudes. Some currents of air can exacerbate the problems associated with other natural events. For example, foehn winds often aggravate wildfires in southern California or cause the sudden melting of the snow pack on mountains.

Despite being agents of death and destruction, tornadoes, tropical cyclones, and other violent winds are atmospheric mechanisms designed to move heat energy from regions with a surplus to regions where there is a shortage. This circulation is vital to the healthy function of our atmosphere as one that supports life.

Appendix A:
The Average Composition of the Atmosphere

Gas	Composition by Volume (ppm)*	Composition by Weight (ppm)*	Total Mass (10^{20} g)
nitrogen	780,900	755,100	38.648
oxygen	209,500	231,500	11.841
argon	9,300	12,800	0.655
carbon dioxide	386	591	0.0299
neon	18	12.5	0.000636
helium	5.2	0.72	0.000037
methane	1.5	0.94	0.000043
krypton	1.0	2.9	0.000146
nitrous oxide	0.5	0.8	0.000040
hydrogen	0.5	0.035	0.000002
ozone**	0.4	0.7	0.000035
xenon	0.08	0.36	0.000018

*ppm = parts per million.
**Variable, increases with height.

Appendix B:
The Beaufort Scale of Wind (Nautical)

BEAUFORT NUMBER	NAME OF WIND	WIND SPEED		DESCRIPTION OF SEA SURFACE
		KNOTS	KPH	
0	calm	<1	<1	sea like a mirror
1	light air	1–3	1–5	ripples with appearance of scales are formed, without foam crests
2	light breeze	4–6	6–11	small wavelets still short but more pronounced; crests have a glassy appearance but do not break
3	gentle breeze	7–10	12–19	large wavelets; crests begin to break; foam of glassy appearance; perhaps scattered white horses
4	moderate breeze	11–16	20–28	small waves becoming longer; fairly frequent white horses
5	fresh breeze	17–21	29–38	moderate waves taking a more pronounced long form; many white horses are formed; chance of some spray
6	strong breeze	22–27	39–49	large waves begin to form; the white foam crests are more extensive everywhere; probably some spray
7	moderate gale (or near gale)	28–33	50–61	sea heaps up and white foam from breaking waves begins to be blown in streaks along the direction of the wind; spindrift begins to be seen

Beaufort Number	Name of Wind	Wind Speed		Description of Sea Surface
		KNOTS	KPH	
8	fresh gale (or gale)	34–40	62–74	moderately high waves of greater length; edges of crests break into spindrift; foam is blown in well-marked streaks along the direction of the wind
9	strong gale	41–47	75–88	high waves; dense streaks of foam along the direction of the wind; sea begins to roll; spray affects visibility
10	whole gale (or storm)	48–55	89–102	very high waves with long overhanging crests; resulting foam in great patches is blown in dense white streaks along the direction of the wind; on the whole the surface of the sea takes on a white appearance; rolling of the sea becomes heavy; visibility affected
11	storm (or violent storm)	56–63	103–114	exceptionally high waves; small- and medium-sized ships might be for a long time lost to view behind the waves; sea is covered with long white patches of foam; everywhere the edges of the wave crests are blown into foam; visibility affected
12–17	hurricane	64 and above	117 and above	the air is filled with foam and spray; sea is completely white with driving spray; visibility very seriously affected

Beaufort Number	Sea Disturbance Number	Average Wave Height	
		FT	M
0	0	0	0
1	0	0	0
2	1	0–1	0–0.3
3	2	1–2	0.3–0.6
4	3	2–4	0.6–1.2
5	4	4–8	1.2–2.4
6	5	8–13	2.4–4
7	6	13–20	4–6
8	6	13–20	4–6
9	6	13–20	4–6
10	7	20–30	6–9
11	8	30–45	9–14
12–17	9	over 45	over 14

Appendix C:
The Enhanced Fujita (EF) Scale of Tornado Intensity

This scale was implemented as the standard scale of tornado intensity for the United States on February 1, 2007.

EF NUMBER	WIND SPEED RANGE*			
	METRES PER SECOND	KILOMETRES PER HOUR	FEET PER SECOND	MILES PER HOUR
0	29–38	105–137	95–125	65–85
1	38–49	138–177	126–161	86–110
2	50–60	179–217	163–198	111–135
3	61–74	219–266	199–242	136–165
4	74–89	267–322	243–293	166–200
5	89+	322+	293+	over 200

*Like the Fujita Scale, the Enhanced Fujita Scale is a set of wind estimates (not measurements of wind at the surface). Each level in the Enhanced Fujita Scale is derived from three-second wind gusts estimated at the point of damage to 28 indicators (such as trees, buildings, and various types of infrastructure) and the degree of damage to each indicator. Wind estimates vary with height and exposure. Each value is converted from miles per hour and rounded to the nearest whole number.

Source: Modified from the Enhanced F Scale for Tornado Damage webpage (http://www.spc.noaa.gov/efscale/ef-scale.html), produced by the National Oceanic and Atmospheric Association (NOAA).

Appendix D:
The Saffir-Simpson and Australian Cyclone Scales

SAFFIR-SIMPSON HURRICANE SCALE*				
CATEGORY	WIND SPEED		STORM SURGE		DAMAGE
	MPH	KM/HR	FEET	METRES	
1	74-95	119-154	4-5	1.2-1.5	damage primarily to shrubs, trees, and unanchored mobile homes; inundation of low-lying coastal roads
2	96-110	155-178	6-8	1.8-2.4	considerable damage to shrubs, trees, and exposed mobile homes; coastal roads flooded; piers damaged
3	111-130	179-210	9-12	2.7-3.7	large trees uprooted; mobile homes destroyed; structural damage to small buildings; serious flooding at coast
4	131-155	211-250	13-18	3.9-5.5	shrubs, trees, signs blown down; major damage to roofs and windows and to lower floors of structures near shores
5	>155	>250	>18	>5.5	small buildings blown down; many structures completely unroofed; evacuations necessary 5-10 miles (8-16 km) from coast

*Used to rank tropical cyclones in the North Atlantic Ocean (including the Gulf of Mexico and Caribbean Sea) and the eastern North Pacific Ocean. Published by permission of Herbert Saffir, consulting engineer, and Robert Simpson, meteorologist.

AUSTRALIAN SCALE OF CYCLONE INTENSITY			
CATEGORY	WIND SPEED		DAMAGE
	KM/HR	MPH	
1	63-90	39-56	some damage to crops, trees, caravans (mobile homes); gusts to 125 km/hr (78 mph)
2	91-125	57-78	heavy damage to crops, significant damage to caravans; gusts of 125-170 km/hr (78-105 mph)
3*	126-165	79-102	some caravans destroyed; some roofs and structures damaged; gusts of 170-225 km/hr (105-140 mph)
4	166-226	103-140	significant damage to roofs and structures; caravans destroyed; gusts of 225-280 km/hr (140-174 mph)
5	>226	>140	widespread destruction; gusts greater than 280 km/hr (174 mph)

*Corresponds roughly to category 1 of the Saffir-Simpson hurricane scale.
Source: Commonwealth Bureau of Meteorology.

Appendix E:
Cyclonic Naming Systems

HURRICANE NAMES FOR THE NORTH ATLANTIC OCEAN*					
2005	2006	2007	2008	2009	2010
Arlene	Alberto	Andrea	Arthur	Ana	Alex
Bret	Beryl	Barry	Bertha	Bill	Bonnie
Cindy	Chris	Chantal	Cristobal	Claudette	Colin
Dennis	Debby	Dean	Dolly	Danny	Danielle
Emily	Ernesto	Erin	Edouard	Erika	Earl
Franklin	Florence	Felix	Fay	Fred	Fiona
Gert	Gordon	Gabrielle	Gustav	Grace	Gaston
Harvey	Helene	Humberto	Hanna	Henri	Hermine
Irene	Isaac	Ingrid	Ike	Ida	Igor
Jose	Joyce	Jerry	Josephine	Joaquin	Julia
Katrina	Kirk	Karen	Kyle	Kate	Karl
Lee	Leslie	Lorenzo	Laura	Larry	Lisa
Maria	Michael	Melissa	Marco	Mindy	Matthew
Nate	Nadine	Noel	Nana	Nicholas	Nicole
Ophelia	Oscar	Olga	Omar	Odette	Otto
Philippe	Patty	Pablo	Paloma	Peter	Paula
Rita	Rafael	Rebekah	Rene	Rose	Richard
Stan	Sandy	Sebastien	Sally	Sam	Shary
Tammy	Tony	Tanya	Teddy	Teresa	Tomas
Vince	Valerie	Van	Vicky	Victor	Virginie
Wilma	William	Wendy	Wilfred	Wanda	Walter

*Names are applied in alphabetical order each year. Lists are recycled every six years--names from 2005 reused in 2011 and so on. Names can be retired if used once for exceptional hurricanes.
Source: U.S. National Weather Service, National Hurricane Center.

HURRICANE NAMES FOR THE EASTERN NORTH PACIFIC OCEAN*

2005	2006	2007	2008	2009	2010
Adrian	Aletta	Alvin	Alma	Andres	Agatha
Beatriz	Bud	Barbara	Boris	Blanca	Blas
Calvin	Carlotta	Cosme	Cristina	Carlos	Celia
Dora	Daniel	Dalila	Douglas	Dolores	Darby
Eugene	Emilia	Erick	Elida	Enrique	Estelle
Fernanda	Fabio	Flossie	Fausto	Felicia	Frank
Greg	Gilma	Gil	Genevieve	Guillermo	Georgette
Hilary	Hector	Henriette	Hernan	Hilda	Howard
Irwin	Ileana	Ivo	Iselle	Ignacio	Isis
Jova	John	Juliette	Julio	Jimena	Javier
Kenneth	Kristy	Kiko	Karina	Kevin	Kay
Lidia	Lane	Lorena	Lowell	Linda	Lester
Max	Miriam	Manuel	Marie	Marty	Madeline
Norma	Norman	Narda	Norbert	Nora	Newton
Otis	Olivia	Octave	Odile	Olaf	Orlene
Pilar	Paul	Priscilla	Polo	Patricia	Paine
Ramon	Rosa	Raymond	Rachel	Rick	Roslyn
Selma	Sergio	Sonia	Simon	Sandra	Seymour
Todd	Tara	Tico	Trudy	Terry	Tina
Veronica	Vicente	Velma	Vance	Vivian	Virgil
Wiley	Willa	Wallis	Winnie	Waldo	Winifred
Xina	Xavier	Xina	Xavier	Xina	Xavier
York	Yolanda	York	Yolanda	York	Yolanda
Zelda	Zeke	Zelda	Zeke	Zelda	Zeke

*Names are applied in alphabetical order each year. Lists are recycled every six years--names from 2005 reused in 2011 and so on. Names can be retired if used once for exceptional hurricanes.
Source: U.S. National Weather Service, National Hurricane Center.

CONTRIBUTING COUNTRIES	CYCLE I NAME	CYCLE II NAME	CYCLE III NAME	CYCLE IV NAME	CYCLE V NAME
TYPHOON NAMES FOR THE WESTERN NORTH PACIFIC OCEAN AND THE SOUTH CHINA SEA*					
Cambodia	Damrey	Knog-Rey	Nakri	Krovanh	Sarika
China	Longwang	Yutu	Fengshen	Dujuan	Haima
Democratic People's Republic of Korea	Kirogi	Toraji	Kalmaegi	Maemi	Meari
Hong Kong (China)	Kai-Tak	Man-Yi	Fung-Wong	Choi-Wan	Ma-on
Japan	Tembin	Usagi	Kammuri	Koppu	Tokage
Laos	Bolaven	Pabuk	Phanfone	Ketsana	Nock-ten
Macau	Chanchu	Wutip	Vongfong	Parma	Muifa
Malaysia	Jelawat	Sepat	Rusa	Melor	Merbok
Micronesia	Ewiniar	Fitow	Sinlaku	Nepartak	Nanmadol
Philippines	Bilis	Danas	Hagupit	Lupit	Tals
Republic of Korea	Kaemi	Nari	Changmi	Sudal	Noru
Thailand	Prapiroon	Vipa	Megkhla	Nida	Kularb
U.S.A.	Maria	Francisco	Higos	Omais	Roke
Vietnam	Hoamai	Lekima	Bavi	Conson	Sonca
Cambodia	Bopha	Krosa	Maysak	Chanthu	Nesat
China	Wukong	Haiyan	Haishen	Dianmu	Haitang
Democratic People's Republic of Korea	Sonamu	Podul	Pongsona	Mindulle	Nalgae
Hong Kong (China)	Shanshan	Lingling	Yanyan	Tingting	Banyan
Japan	Yagi	Kajiki	Kujira	Kompasu	Washi
Laos	Xangsane	Faxai	Chan-Hom	Namtheun	Matsa

CONTRIBUTING COUNTRIES	CYCLE I	CYCLE II	CYCLE III	CYCLE IV	CYCLE V
	NAME	NAME	NAME	NAME	NAME
Malaysia	Rumbia	Tapah	Nangka	Meranti	Mawar
Micronesia	Soulik	Mitag	Soudelor	Rananin	Guchol
Philippines	Cimaron	Hagibis	Imbudo	Malakas	Talim
Republic of Korea	Chebi	Noguri	Koni	Megi	Nabi
Thailand	Durian	Ramasoon	Hanuman	Chaba	Khanun
U.S.A.	Utor	Chataan	Etau	Kodo	Vicete
Vietnam	Trami	Halong	Vamco	Songda	Saola

*Names are applied from an entire cycle before proceeding to next cycle, regardless of year. Names submitted by each country range from personal names to descriptive terms to names of animals and plants.

Sources: World Meteorological Organization; U.S. Dept. of Defense, Joint Typhoon Warning Center

GLOSSARY

adiabatic Having to do with a process that takes place without any exchange (loss or gain) of heat.

anemometer An instrument for measuring and indicating the force and velocity of the wind.

annulus A part, structure, or marking resembling a ring.

convective That which transfers heat by the circulation of a fluid that has a nonuniform temperature due to its density and the action of gravity.

cyclostrophic wind Describes the concentric motion of air within a tropical cyclone when the two main forces acting on an air parcel are the centripetal force and the pressure-gradient force.

dropsonde A radiosonde—a miniature radio transmitter with instruments for broadcasting the humidity, temperature, and pressure—dropped by parachute from a high-flying airplane.

insolation Solar radiation that has been received by a surface or the rate of delivery of direct solar radiation per unit of a horizontal surface.

isothermal Having to do with equality of temperature.

katabatic Having to do with an air current or wind moving downward or down a slope because of cooling, especially at night.

laminar flow Streamlined flow in a fluid near a solid boundary.

mesocyclone A region of wind rotation, around 3.2–9.7 kilometres (2–6 miles) in diameter and often found in the back right of a supercell storm.

noctilucent Shining or glowing at night, especially of very high-altitude clouds that reflect sunlight long after sunset.

occluded front A weather front cut off from contact with the surface of Earth and forced aloft by the convergence of a cold front with a warm front.

rime Granular ice tufts that accumulate on the windward sides of exposed objects that is formed from supercooled fog or clouds and built out directly against the wind.

shearing Internal force tangential to the section on which is is acting; or applied forces causing two contiguous parts of a body to slide relative to one another in a direction parallel to their plane of contact.

synoptic scale The scale of weather occurring over a horizontal regions in excess of 1,000 kilometres (620 miles).

thermocline A layer in a thermally stratified body of water that separates an upper, warmer, lighter, oxygen-rich zone from a lower, colder, heavier, oxygen-poor zone.

tropopause The upper boundary of the troposphere, which is usually characterized by an abrupt change in lapse rate from positive, or decreasing temperature with height, to neutral or negative, or temperature that remains constant or increases with height.

BIBLIOGRAPHY

Tornadoes

A personal account of field research on tornadic thunderstorms is presented by Howard B. Bluestein, *Tornado Alley: Monster Storms of the Great Plains* (1999), an easy-to-read work that presents a clear discussion of the origin and effects of a tornado and includes numerous dramatic photographs. Documentation of all strong and violent tornadoes in the United States since the 1950s, as well as information on the risk of a strong or violent tornado at a particular location, is provided by Thomas P. Grazulis, *Significant Tornadoes, 1680–1991* (1993) and its update *Significant Tornadoes Update, 1992–1995* (1997). While aimed at a technical audience, these works are moderately easy to read and contain much information of general interest.

T. Theodore Fujita, *U.S. Tornadoes. Part One* (1987–98), by the "grand master" of tornado research in the United States for many years, covers tornado climatology of the 20th century. A basic, easy-to-read report on how tornadic winds produce damage is provided by Joseph E. Minor, *The Tornado: An Engineering-Oriented Perspective* (1978, reprinted 1993). Information is also included on how some damage can be mitigated by good construction practices.

Basic information on every severe weather event in the United States is compiled monthly from reports submitted by National Weather Service offices and presented by the National Oceanic and Atmospheric Administration in the periodical *Storm Data*; feature articles are presented on particularly notable events. Edwin Kessler (ed.),

Thunderstorms: A Social, Scientific, and Technological Documentary, 2nd ed. rev. and enlarged, 3 vol. (1983–88), provides extensive coverage of tornadoes as well as hail, damaging straight-line winds, and lightning. Written for a wide audience, the individual articles range from easily accessible to highly technical.

TROPICAL CYCLONES

A general overview of the physical mechanisms of tropical cyclone formation and behaviour, with particular emphasis on Hurricane Andrew of 1992, is presented by Roger A. Pielke, Sr., and Roger A. Pielke, Jr., *Hurricanes: Their Nature and Impacts on Society* (1997). John M. Williams and Iver W. Duedall, *Florida Hurricanes and Tropical Storms* (1997), discusses tropical storms and cyclones affecting Florida since 1871. A classic work on the structure and mechanics of tropical cyclones is Gordon E. Dunn and Banner I. Miller, *Atlantic Hurricanes*, rev. ed. (1964). C. Donald Ahrens, *Meteorology Today*, 6th ed. (1999), is an introductory textbook containing a chapter on tropical cyclones.

The formation and tracking of Hurricane Gilbert is recorded in *Hurricane!* (1989), a video documentary produced for the American Public Broadcasting Service's *NOVA* series. *Hurricanes* (1998), produced for the History Channel's *Wrath of God* series, provides footage of three great cyclones that struck the United States in the 20th century.

A technically advanced discussion of all aspects of tropical cyclones is given by Gary R. Foley, Hugh E. Willoughby, John L. McBride, Russell L. Elsberry, Isaac Ginis, and L. Chien, *Global Perspectives on Tropical Cyclones*, published by World Meteorological Organization (1995). Also at an advanced level, the factors controlling variability of Atlantic hurricanes, seasonal and long-term forecasts, and the impact of hurricanes on the insurance industry is presented by James B. Elsner and A. Birol Kara, *Hurricanes of the North Atlantic: Climate and Society* (1999).

THE ATMOSPHERE

General references on meteorology, climatology, and aeronomy are provided in Ira W. Geer (ed.), *Glossary of Weather and Climate: With Related Oceanic and Hydrologic Terms* (1996). Introductory texts for meteorology and climatology include Edward Aguado and James E. Burt, *Understanding Weather and Climate*, 4th ed. (2007); Frederick K. Lutgens and Edward J. Tarbuck, *The Atmosphere: An Introduction to Meteorology*, 10th ed. (2007); C. Donald Ahrens, *Meteorology Today: An Introduction to Weather, Climate, and the Environment*, 8th ed. (2007); Roger G. Barry and Richard J. Chorley, *Atmosphere, Weather, and Climate*, 8th ed. (2003); Joseph M. Moran, Michael D. Morgan, and Patricia M. Pauley, *Meteorology: The Atmosphere and the Science of Weather*, 5th ed. (1997); Lee M. Grenci and Jon M. Nese, *A World of Weather: Fundamentals of Meteorology*, 4th ed. (2006); Richard A. Anthes, *Meteorology*, 7th ed. (1997); Eric W. Danielson, James Levin, and Elliot Abrams, *Meteorology*, 2nd ed. (2003); and Dennis L. Hartmann, *Global Physical Climatology* (1994). Books that portray the role of the atmosphere within the climate system include William R. Cotton and Roger A. Pielke, Sr., *Human Impacts on Weather and Climate* (2007); and P. Kabat et al. (eds.), *Vegetation, Water, Humans, and the Climate: A New Perspective on an Interactive System* (2004).

INDEX